The Civilian Conservation Corps & the Building of Guernsey State Park
With Folktales and Stories of the Park

Neil A. Waring

Old Trails Publishing
Wyoming USA

http://oldtrailspublishing.blogspot.com

Enjoy The Park!

Neil A. Waring

Old Trails Publishing

http://oldtrailspublishing.blogspot.com

To my wife Jan, whose constant encouragement and great knowledge of the park, and park history, kept me researching and plugging away to the finish.

The Civilian Conservation Corps & the Building of Guernsey State Park

With Folktales and Stories of the Park

Table of Contents

Preface

I have not attempted with this book to write a complete history of the Civilian Conservation Corps or of Guernsey State Park. A complete history would need to be much more comprehensive than my work. This book instead, looks at only a portion, yet most important part of CCC history, the history of the CCC and the building of Guernsey Lake into Guernsey State Park. This is the story of that project.

The CCC was an intriguing organization, much needed during a most interesting time in American history. A time between the wars, depression time. I did not attempt to politicize the CCC as to whether it was good or bad for the nation, or to the long lasting consequences of the New Deal programs.

The building of the park was important, and remains important to the history and economy of south-east, Wyoming. In the writing of this book I have separated the works of the two Civilian Conservation Corps camps from work done previously by the Bureau of Reclamation. It was my goal to include all the important projects and events that were such a large part of the Civilian Conservation Corps, and others, in the building of Guernsey Lake State Park.

My wish is for readers to absorb some of the flavor of the life and times of the CCC. It is also my intention to tell some of the great pre-CCC stories of the park. Stories, most of them only oral history, now beginning to fade away, stories that need to be preserved in print.

History, as a record, regularly deals with large movements and happenings, but it is sometimes the smaller local histories that delve deeper into events and their time and place as a part of history. Much of history is people remembering, telling stories of experiences, and of time and place. When I found myself deep into the research for this project I felt more and more connected to the Civilian Conservation Corps. Now, so many years removed from the days of the CCC, only a handful of workers are still alive to tell their stories. As of the writing of this book the average age of living former CCC workers was 97.

After finishing this history I hope readers will get a feel for what life was like as part of the CCC in the 1930s, Wyoming. This work deals with actual events, places and people, except for the two short works of fiction based on tales of actual camp happenings. Everything in this book is based on research compiled through the examination of stories, diaries, and writings of others, and my many decades as a classroom teacher. The best part of putting together this book were the countless eventful trips to the park.

When built, Guernsey State Park was an experiment. A first of its kind combined effort between the Bureau of Reclamation and the National Park Service. It was an experiment in taking a new North Platte River reservoir, built for irrigation and hydroelectric power, and turning it into a recreation area and park that everyone could enjoy. In addition, it was an experiment in Park architecture, newly coined as Parkitecture, a unique effort to blend nature into building. How did it work? Take a look around.

Guernsey State Park, a recreationalist's and nature lover's paradise. A park that today is nearly the same, and every bit as functional, as when built by the Civilian Conservation Corps 80 years ago.

The Narrows

Acknowledgments

Several years ago the state of Wyoming ran an advertising campaign with the slogan, "Wyoming, Like No Place on Earth." The campaign has long ago passed into memory, but for those who've visited Guernsey State Park it could well read, Guernsey State Park, Like No Place on Earth.

The Park offers wonderful mountain vistas, trails, picnic shelters, deep blue water, history and breath taking beauty. How could anyone ask for more? Spend a few hours or a day or two in the park and enjoy this place where history and nature cross paths.

Many Thanks to everyone for their encouragement helping to make this project a reality.

© Neil A. Waring 2014

Introduction

Guernsey State Park features an abundance of well-preserved work by the Civilian Conservation Corps. When building the park, CCC workers were told they were building something for the ages. Prophetic today.

Guernsey State Park Museum

On the east side of the park, the Museum, many superb picnic shelters, and Lakeshore Drive remain as monuments to the skill and ingenuity of the builders of the Civilian Conservation Corps. Skyline Drive, on the west side of the park, takes visitors to places not accessible before the engineers and workers of the Civilian Conservation Corps arrived in Guernsey. The Castle on the North

Bluff at the end of Skyline Drive is a massive stone and log shelter often referred to as the most elaborate picnic shelter in America.

Observation, Lookout at the Castle on the North Bluff

Dozens of other buildings, roads, trails, culverts, retaining walls and bridges built by the CCC can be seen throughout the park. The park itself is not only a fine history lesson of the Civilian Conservation Corps, but of building parks and recreational facilities throughout America. If that is not enough for history buffs, the Oregon and Mormon Trails pass on either side of the park.

On September 25, 1997 Lake Guernsey State Park was designated a National Historic Landmark. This followed the 1981 designation of the Dam, Gatehouse and Powerplant on the Historic Register.

The most recent nomination forms followed the history of the CCC workers in the park. The designation was well deserved and much credit and thanks are given by this author to the research efforts and hard work of those people who made the National Landmark status possible.

This account covers, in some small way, the goings on, lives and legends of the CCC and the many young men who built the park. In his wonderful book, *Cowboy Life: Reconstructing an American Myth*, William Savage Jr. said, "Most real life cowboys were just that—boys between 18 and 25. Unwilling to stay at home with pasture and plow, they became hired hands on horseback, most did not even own their own horses and few rose above their humble station."*

The men of the CCC, most also in the 18-25, age group represented that same Cowboy spirit 50 years later. Young men too restless to stay at home. It was Depression time in America, but young men still needed purpose, they needed to find themselves, they needed space and time, some needed to wander, each needed work. These men, even if it was but for a brief time, rose above their humble station in life, they were the hard working men of the Civilian Conservation Corps.

Perhaps Owen Wister said it best in his classic Wyoming tale, *The Virginian*, "Well, he will be here among us always, invisible, waiting his chance to live and play as he would like. His wild kind has been among us always, since the beginning: a young man with his temptations, a hero without wings."*

This book stands as a tribute to those working men of the CCC. Young men, who dreamed, sweated, played and grew up during a brief time of their lives in Guernsey, Wyoming. Their kind has always been with us, with us for a little while, who then like Wister's cowboy, wandered off into the pages of history. In the few years the men of the CCC labored in Guernsey they turned a Bureau of Reclamation, irrigation and hydroelectric dam on the North Platte River into the beautiful, Guernsey State Park.

Often, these invisible people of history are hard to find. Workers, they came, they built, and they left, to go on with their lives. When one looks closely, their kind has truly always been with us.

Although historical in nature, this work was not intended to be a pure, research based study, but instead meant to be lighthearted and easy reading, a telling of both the old and the new stories of the park. Learning about history can be fun and exciting; reading history doesn't have to be dull and mind-numbing.

Guernsey State Park is blessed with a rich history, much of it made by the Civilian Conservation Corps. The pages of this book will also reveal bits of the parks rich history from the time before the CCC.

Enjoy your read!

Neil A. Waring- 2015

Chapter 1 – The Beginning

Happy Days are Here Again

"It is my belief that what is being accomplished will conserve our natural resources, create future national wealth and approve of moral and spiritual value not only to those of you who are taking part, but to the rest of the country as well. You young men who are enrolled in this work are to be congratulated as well. It is my honest conviction that what you are doing in the way of constructive service will bring you, personally and individually, returns the value of which it is difficult to estimate.

FDR Addresses the Press

Physically fit, as demonstrated by the examinations you took before entering the camps, the clean life and hard work in which you are engaged cannot fail to help your physical condition and you should emerge from this experience strong and rugged and ready for reentrance into the ranks of industry, better equipped than before. Opportunities for employment in work for which individually you are best suited are increasing daily and you should emerge from this experience splendidly equipped for the competitive fields of endeavor which always mark the industrial life Of America.[1]

With those words the Civilian Conservation Corps became a reality under the New Deal and Guernsey Lake State Park would also become a reality.

Franklin Delano Roosevelt became America's 32nd president on March 4, 1933. FDR, as the nation knew him, got off to a fast start his first 100 days in office. Roosevelt pushed through dozens of executive orders and pressed for quick congressional passage of bills grouped together to create the New Deal.

Roosevelt's New Deal was a file cabinet full of programs with one common goal; pull America out of the Great Depression. The programs were designed to produce economic growth through job creation, relief through government jobs, and reform with new regulations for transportation, banking, and Wall Street. Unquestionably, the centerpiece of all the New Deal programs was Social Security and its long reaching benefits to the nation's retired citizens.

But the Civilian Conservation Corps and the jobs it would create was, indisputably, FDR's favorite of the programs created within the framework of the New Deal. He was excited to have a program fitting the two things he held most dear, tremendous environmental benefits with the preservation of many of our nations natural resources. It also helped put together a jobs program, the human resource element, so needed in a depression locked America.

One month into his term, on March 31, 1933 Roosevelt got the CCC up and running. On that day he signed into law Public No. 5, after it had been passed by the seventy-third congress. His signature created what was then called the ECW or Emergency Conservation Works. The ECW soon became the better known CCC, Civilian Conservation Corps. Throughout America newspapers referred to the beginnings of the CCC as, "Roosevelt's Tree Army," possibly because of the tree logo used by the CCC, or because of work, yet to be done, in western forested lands involving the planting of millions of trees.

In his notes, J. H. Coffman, Camp BR-9 Superintendent, accounts for the planting of more than 500 trees in the park.[2]

Natural Old Growth Forest in the Park

Other camp diaries mention planting trees and shrubs near the Museum. Early photos of the Museum show the steps going from the lower parking area to the Museum with no trees in sight. If any natural vegetation was present workers removed it to build the great rock steps leading to the Museum. Today it is hard to tell which trees were planted around the park and what trees are old growth products of Mother Nature.

Trees are difficult to grow in Wyoming and the tree planters of the Civilian Conservation Corps left a legacy of new trees in the park and all across America. Although now lost from old age, one of the most interesting tree plantings in the park was the placing of several apple trees at the low point of Red Cliff Trail near the end of a long flight of rustic rock steps.

Museum Steps

Like all the buildings in the park, trees were planted in harmony with nature, to blend in and not stand out. Only on the old CCC built golf course can one readily see trees in a straight line, obviously planted by the Civilian Conservation Corps. Unlike some CCC projects, trees and shrubs at Guernsey were not brought in. They were dug up along the lake and river then moved around the park.

Although there was no actual count of trees planted in the park, reports vary from 500 to as high as 5,000.

If it was the latter number, it likely included shrubs planted around park structures.

CCC Golf Course-photo from Spotted Tail Mountain

Pines, CCC Planted, Near the Museum

Is Guernsey State Park part of the famous Roosevelt Tree Army of the CCC? Indeed it is!

Wyoming had 136 Civilian Conservation Corps camps of which only 13 were Bureau of Reclamation Camps. Both Guernsey camps, Company No. 844, most often referred to as camp BR-9 and Company No. 1858 or BR-10 were Bureau of Reclamation camps. Of the 136 camps in Wyoming, 55 were in or near Yellowstone. Only four camps were in the far eastern part of the state, one in Veteran, formed from Guernsey's camp BR-10, one in Douglas and the two in Guernsey.[3]

The CCC looked for unemployed and unmarried citizens at least 18 and not over 26 years of age. Young men were signed-up or enlisted for a period of six months. Re-enlistment was an option and many decided to stay for extra time in the corps. Re-enlistments were limited to three, after the initial enrollment, allowing a man to serve a maximum of two years in the organization.

Civilian Conservation Corps laborers were paid $30 a month. After a successful start, some vocational and educational opportunities were available to the enrollees. From 1933 to 1942 the CCC employed over three million young men. At Guernsey State Park the CCC was active from May of 1934 until August of 1938, and employed well over 1,000 of the 36,000 thousand workers who served the Corps in Wyoming.[4]

Some Americans, looking at the CCC from the outside, believed it was something romantic, especially looking at the adventure of working in the west. Work in a park like Guernsey seemed to early CCC men, many from the American South, Southwest, and a few from the East Coast, to be a job on the last of the American frontier.

Many other places, especially in the west, gave early enrollees a chance to see the country. In the case of what would be named, Guernsey Lake State Park, a chance to work in a location that must have seemed to 1930s city dwellers a virgin wilderness.

One of many small mountains in the park

As the CCC grew, the work force became more and more local. No longer were city boys being turned into western cowboys. In later sign-up periods workers came from throughout Wyoming and surrounding states.

By July of 1933, the CCC reached 300,000 men. It grew by another 40,000 by the end of the year and within two years it reached its zenith of over 600,000 men. Indeed, by 1936 the corps seemed to be working so well that debates in Washington centered on how to give it a permanent place in America. But it wouldn't last. The corps was gradually whittled back to 340,000 men lasting until WWII.

Roosevelt hoped the idea of the CCC would become popular throughout the country. His hopes came true far beyond what even the optimistic FDR dreamed. Within a year both political parties and a majority of Americans were quite happy with the CCC.

The *Boston Evening Transcript* went so far as to say, "In the main, from the start, this army of conservation has shown itself to be well disciplined and efficient in its work, and it has apparently maintained a commendable standard of conduct in its leisure hours."[5]

For many people in America the Civilian Conservation Corps became the first great American dream. Of all the original New Deal programs the CCC has had the most long lasting effects. It was an excellent program, one needed in its time and place, but World War II changed all of that. The war effort needed money and men. The CCC used lots of government money and had countless young men. Thus the Civilian Conservation Corps unceremoniously and abruptly ended as America became involved in World War II.

Roosevelt went on to introduce Social Security and the Works Progress Administration (WPA) as part of a second New Deal. Over the next decade plus FDR would win four presidential elections serving a bit over 12 years before dying in office shortly after being elected to an unprecedented fourth term. His legacy to America will be the Social Security system, but for anyone who has visited Guernsey State Park, his legacy just might be the great work of hundreds of Civilian Conservation Corps young men who helped put in place recreational and cultural opportunities. These are continuing in their grander and use more than three quarters of a century later.

Lakeshore Drive View of Laramie Peak

The Drive was built, not only for great views of the lake, but of the mountains within and surrounding the park.

Chapter 2 – The East Side

Camp BR-9

Two Civilian Conservation Corps camps were inside the boundaries of Guernsey State Park, Camp BR-9, south of the Museum on the east side, and camp BR-10, south off Skyline Drive on the west side of the lake. The two camps would be assigned the job of turning Guernsey Dam into a recreation paradise. Today sightseers, boaters, hikers, campers, wildlife watchers, history buffs, photographers and others would heartily agree their mission was accomplished.

Camp RS-1, the first Civilian Conservation Corps Reclamation Camp, soon became Camp BR-9, the first North Platte River Project camp in Wyoming. The camp was established May 21, 1934, during the third enrolment period for workers.

The new camp was a multiple joint project between the Bureau of Reclamation and the National Park Service. It was, along with a project in New Mexico, the first of many joint efforts of the Park Service and the CCC.[6] When the CCC came to Guernsey, the lake was seven years old with few recreational offerings. The Bureau of Reclamation built Guernsey Dam, now one of five Wyoming reservoirs on the North Platte River. Although the dam at Guernsey was in place, the lack of recreation afforded the perfect blank canvas for the planners from the National Park

Service, along with the perfect opportunity for the hard working men of the CCC.

Camp BR-9, circa, 1936

Photo - Wyoming State Archives, Department of State Parks and Cultural Resources

Camp BR-9 was created out of Company No. 844, a U.S. Forest Service camp located in Fort Bliss, Texas.[7] The ever changing group of men of camp BR-9 would spend the next 51 months working on park projects. The camp was set on a bluff above the North Platte River overlooking the dam and Powerplant.

What's left of the camp today can be reached by taking the Museum road, part way up where the road steepens and bends to the left an old gated trail road travels on east or to the driver's right. This old trail leads to the remains of Company

844s, Camp BR-9. The area is being used for park storage and has been for many years.

This camp also served as the home of the National Park Service headquarters, housed in a building that had been an early project of BR-9. The camp area and remaining buildings can be seen today from the bluff immediately south of the Museum parking lot.

Almost before the men were settled into the tents being used until permanent quarters could be built, they were called to fight a forest fire. In 1934 alone the men of Company 844 would fight six different forest fires.[8]   By the time the CCC came to an end,   throughout America the men of the CCC had spent six and a half million man days fighting forest fires.[9] They were so effective fighting the fires that the period of the CCC remains one of the lowest destructive forest fire periods in American history. Many projects were tackled by the two camps at Guernsey but always they were on call to fight fires. No matter the project, when the fire calls came, the men were loaded up in trucks, complete with hand tools, and taken to the hot spots.[10]

The first year, in all camps, work included the building of permanent structures for the men and offices for the company. At Lake Guernsey, the CCC employees were no different, laboring away the first year on more permanent wood structures used for both living and storage.   Unfortunately today, only two of the original 22 buildings of the camp still stand. Both of these buildings were part of the original Camp BR-9.

The remaining buildings are readily visible from the south edge of the Museum parking lot and nearby walking trails. The two buildings were originally a blacksmith/machinery repair shop and a ten stall garage the CCC called the truck garage.

Camp BR-9 Blacksmith Shop/Garage as it Looks Today

The two buildings are wood frame and appear to be in decent condition considering their age and constant use since the middle 1930s.

A careful study of this area finds trail heads and visible evidence of the original campsite including old foundations and walk paths. Although this area is gated off from park visitors, well-marked walking trails pass within a few yards of the old camp allowing history buffs a nice view, along with the opportunity to photograph the two building left behind in old Camp BR-9.

The Ten Stall Garage of Camp-9

Like many government projects, the planners of Guernsey State Park ran out of time and money before they ran out of ideas, and well before all of the wished for projects were completed. World War II, already raging in Europe, may also have had something to do with the unfinished projects. Graded and staked lots for leasable lake shore homes grew into flat areas of buffalo grass. A superintendent's residence, park lodge and an even more extensive trail system were other projects left on the drawing boards at CCC camp headquarters.

The CCC Tennis Court

Some projects were completed but are no longer part of the recreational offerings of the park.

CCC Tennis Courts

Photo Wyoming State Archives, Department of State Parks and Cultural Resources

Two distinct features of the early park are invisible, or almost so, today. Where the Museum parking lot now welcomes dozens of cars every day once was a tennis court.

Yes, a CCC tennis court. Nothing remains today not even the knowledge of how long the tennis court was used, or when the nets and final fencing were removed. The best guess is that when the workers left, so did the demand for tennis courts at Lake Guernsey. The court soon deteriorated and the scenic road around Round Top Mountain was finished and became the popular choice for getting to the Museum. After that, the tennis court became the upper parking lot.

Now we have but memories of the courts. If a person listens really hard, on one of those, only in the park, clear as a bell summer evenings, maybe, just maybe, you will once again hear the footsteps and the thud, thud, thud of tennis balls. Nightfall might bring muted laughter of young men, muffled by eight decades of silence, playing tennis, happy with their life in the CCC camp. Full stomachs and a little money in their pockets, a hard day of work behind and recreation before a deep and relaxing sleep. Life could be good for the men of the CCC.

The park today, minus the court, is well known for other types of outdoor recreation, particularly hiking, biking, and animal and bird watching, along with picnicking, camping and water recreation.

I'm not sure anyone misses the old Camp-9 tennis court today but it does make for an interesting story.

CCC Golf Course

The working men of Camp BR-9 also built a nine-hole golf course. The course was complete with tee boxes built inside carefully placed rock perimeters, and nine, oiled sand, greens. The course appears short by today's standards but in the 1930s, using hickory shafted clubs and the brand new, Tommy Armour golf ball, the length would have been fine. The feature hole on the course is number six with a tee box facing west affording a magnificent view of Laramie Peak above the green.

The Author takes a swing decades after the CCC golf course was abandoned.

Number 6 Tee Box

Course construction appears to have been a rather short term project. No earth was moved for the fairways. Tee boxes were built by placing large, basketball size, rocks around the perimeter and then filling the center with a mixture of dirt, stone chips and local clay. All of the tee boxes appear to be less than 50 square feet, but they were of a size considered appropriate for the time when the course was built.

To build the sand greens, prairie sod was removed in circles and a mixture of used motor oil and diesel fuel was spread to treat the ground. The sand green was a mixture of local blow sand and used motor oil. Sand greens are still in use, in this day and age, in a few dry climate states. The only difference is today the sand is mixed with vegetable oil not used motor oil.

Remains of a CCC built Sand Green

Fairways were mown as close as possible allowing for the small rocks and ground hugging gravel make-up of the land. One mowing each month or two during the summer would have kept the course in good condition for play. Unlike the close cropped fairways of today's courses these fairway would have been mowed at three to four inches in height and livestock may have also been allowed to trim the course.

Playing the Feature Hole

Recent historians and viewers of the course have stated the course might be too far gone to rebuild. This could not be further from the truth.

This course was nothing like the pristine courses of today, instead it was rough, and likely took only a few weeks with a handful of men to build. Instead of being difficult to recreate, this course would be rather simple to bring back to its 1937 standards.

It resembled then, and still today bears a resemblance to the courses of Scotland, it was built as a links course, using nature instead of bulldozers to shape the course. Players on courses such as this, played, what is today, sometimes called, winter rules golf, allowing players to lift, clean and place the ball before each shot. Indeed, some players of the 30s used the all new wooden tee for each shot. By playing the sometimes maligned, winter rules, players did not have to hit through rocks or stand in cactus or yucca.

To reach the golf course take the Museum road, approximately half way up, to a large, open, green gate. There is a small pull off on the left (east) and a trail road. This trail leads a half mile to the parking lot for the golf course. The parking area is unrecognizable but looking closely there is a faint drive continuing up to some scrub cedar. This is the location of the golf course parking lot.

The trail road has been barricaded and closed, off and on, over the years, but visitors can always make the hike on the old road in. The walk is easy with little elevation change and is a good choice, even if the road is open, unless your vehicle is a high center of gravity four wheel drive. Pickups and full size SUVs will have no trouble with the ruts in the road. Remember to stay only on the path until you are on foot. No driving is allowed anywhere in the park except on designated roads.

No roads cross the golf course. The trail that is now visible was used by ranchers, fire fighters and park personal but crosses the historically significant golf course and is now used only in emergencies. The last significant use of the road was during the devastating 2012 summer park fire.

The course is covered with small rocks and gravel, prickly pear cactus and yucca are also nearly everywhere on the course. It does not appear the fairways were ever planted, instead they were mowed and left native, cactus, yucca, sagebrush and all. In some places it looks as if the fairways were scraped and then allowed to grow back naturally.

Conception of CCC Golf Course Sign

If grass of any type was planted, it would have been a mixture of common pasture grasses and buffalo grass. Years of allowing nature to reclaim the course make it difficult to distinguish natural grasses from what might have been planted eighty year ago.

With careful searching amateur archeologists can find remnants of tee boxes and changed vegetation patterns signaling long since vanished, used motor oil treated, sand greens.

As late as the middle 1980s there were still a few putting cups and pieces of course signs, and at least one sand-green rake. All seem now to have been either sacrificed to nature or in the hands of artifact collectors. A word of warning- if you happen on a golf ball while walking the course it is most likely a newer model, not a ball from the days of the Civilian Conservation Corps. My reasoning on this thought. It is likely one I lost. Help yourself if it still is white and shiny.

Note – *Many objects found in the park are of historical importance and cannot be removed. Anything found relating to the old CCC golf course, much like Indian artifacts, is significantly important and should be reported to park personnel and left as is and never removed.*

The golf course was officially abandoned sometime in the early 1940s but appears to have had some life for many years after the CCC left. Although no maintenance was done by the state park service, golfers continued to sporadically use the course, or parts of it, well into the 1950s.

In more recent times a few adventurous golfers have hit balls on various parts of the course to see what it may have been like back in 1936.

The last known use of the course for its intended purposes was likely in 1991 when this author enjoyed hitting two balls around the entire nine-hole layout. I tried it again hitting some shots on the course in March of 2014, but was no longer able to visually determine where all of the tees and greens were located.

I found no records of a specific name for the course, and indeed it is probable it was never given a name. I call it Camp BR-9 Links at Guernsey Lake, in my notes. Old fashioned, but I think, a perfect fit.

So, who used the course? It's probable this was to be the boss's playground. Big shots from the CCC, Bureau of Reclamation, National Park Service, and the U.S. Government, plus state and local dignitaries and those who believed they were dignitaries and later many locals enjoyed playing the course.

Original notes on the course stated the city of Guernsey would be part of the building.[11] It doesn't look like they did any work with the CCC on this, other than the possible loan of some city equipment. Local golfers did use and enjoy the course for many years after the CCC camps were gone.

The golf course, evidently, was not out of bounds *(blatant attempt at golf humor)* to the workers, but no records show clubs or balls available for use, making it unlikely the laboring men of BR-9 spent time playing golf. Although golf course building wasn't one of the most known aspects of CCC work, courses were built in other states. It is possible, since the first men of BR-9 came from Texas, where the Corps built several courses, this may have had some bearing on the decision to build a golf course on the east boundary of the park.

Over the past three decades there has been on and off talk of re-doing the BR-9 Golf Links but nothing has come of it. Today, enough remains that the course could be restored to the same condition and look of the BR-9 camp course. As the men of the CCC fade into the footnotes of history, there needs to be an urgency to preserve tangible evidence of this amazing time for thousands of young men.

The Main Boat Dock

Tennis and golf in the park may be only memories today but as some things disappear, others last. The east side of the lake has many CCC projects, most still in remarkable shape, thanks to the good care and upkeep from the state park system. The main boat ramp, less than a half mile upstream from the dam, is a fine example of using available terrain to create outstanding architectural projects. The gravel boat ramp and graded dirt and hard packed gravel parking area were nothing special, the perfect location however, was.

East Side Boat Dock
Photo - Wyoming State Archives, Department of State Parks and Cultural Resources

A tourist might spend hours driving the shore lines of the lake and not find a more perfect spot to launch a boat than the location found by the planners of the Corps eighty years ago.

The CCC also built a group of small, floating, wooden docks, where tourists and locals alike sunbathed, swam, and worked on their diving skills. They have long since wasted away by water and Wyoming weather, but were a terrific attraction many years ago. These areas have been replaced in modern days by town swimming pools with life guards and a much safer, although less picturesque, swimming environment.

Water sports enthusiasts come from much of Southeastern Wyoming along with water sports fanatics from Colorado, Nebraska and occasionally a passerby from other states.

The Stone Fountain

Across Lakeshore Drive from the boat launching area is one of the original BR-9 built drinking fountains. Built by drilling through a huge bolder the fountain is a one of a kind in the park.

Stone Drinking Fountain

New Log Marker with Fountain in the Rock Behind

The drinking fountain itself, with the pipe coming through a large rock, hand drilled by the CCC, is still in good working order and used daily during the warmer months.

East Side Shelters

The three east side picnic shelters, Spotted Tail, Sitting Bull and Red Cloud have been well preserved, holding on to their originality and the building heritage of the Civilian Conservation Corps. With huge, park quarried stone fireplaces, and hand crafted log tables and benches, these areas are like no others in Wyoming State Parks.

The Gambrel roofed, log and stone – Drinking Fountain and Fresh Water Station at Lower Spotted Tail

Many visitors find the most impressive CCC work in the park was the use of massive peeled logs. These huge logs hold up shelter roofs, brace tables and seats and support the four corners of the fresh water station at lower Spotted Tail.

Logs were also used as safety edging for much of the original road work in the park. They barricaded traffic out of unsafe areas and long stretches of log rails lined dangerous curves along Lakeshore Drive. The original log rails have long since been replaced with steel. Today the steel has rusted to the hue of the original log.

Sitting Bull Shelter

It is possible the Civilian Conservation Corps built shelters in Guernsey State Park may be some of the most photographed picnic shelters in America. Sitting Bull shelter is the most elaborate of the east side picnic shelters, built with a huge fire place, stone benches and great views it is the highlight of Lakeshore Drive shelters. Sitting Bull has long been one of the most popular day use picnic areas in the park.

The Shelter at Red Cloud

Red Cloud shelter along with the benches and tables within have been extensively repaired and rebuilt over the years. The shelter still stands in its original, shape, style and size. Amenities inside have also been redone with great respect for the originals.

This shelter area, like the other east side picnic areas, offers both public and secluded areas along with many great views of the lake and of Powell Mountain and Brimmer Point across the water.

Massive Fireplace near Red Cloud Shelter

Upper and Lower Spotted Tail

Spotted Tail has two popular camping and picnicking areas, Upper and Lower, Spotted Tail.

The two shelters at Lower Spotted Tail are simply built and efficient but do not show as much long lasting Civilian Conservation Corps work as other shelters on the east side of the park. The drinking fountain at Lower Spotted Tail is an impressive piece of CCC work. The fountain features, hand carved, stone catch basins that may be one of a kind anywhere in America.

The perfect layout of the locations, the huge peeled log drinking fountain shelter and a rather nice, smaller shelter, showcase CCC work at Lower Spotted Tail.

CCC Water Station at Lower Spotted Tail - View of the peeled timber inside roof structure

Upper Spotted Tail, a popular, away from the water camping area, has only a drive, parking area and bolder work from the CCC.

The two campgrounds at Spotted Tail are much desired destination camping spots. They are not only close to the water but also the starting point for several popular east side hiking trails.

The two campgrounds are separated by Lakeshore Drive with Upper Spotted Tail on the east side and Lower Spotted Tail on the west.

CCC Red Stone fireplace at Spotted Tail

East Side Hiking Trails

A few steps across the road from the peeled log drinking fountain is the starting point for the Evergreen Glade Trail. This trail was built by the CCC and, at the time named, Red Cloud Trail. Today it has been renamed and is a combination of several older trails.

The majority of the new Evergreen Glade Trail and the Museum Trail still follow the original, through the pines, routing of the CCC built Red Cloud Trail. The path retains some of the original rock steps. A modern day touch to this trail has been the addition of interpretive signs drawing attention to and explaining various plants and points of interest along the trail, very nice for new park visitors.

Evergreen Glade - Trail Head at Spotted Tail

Names in the Park

How, why and what places are named can often be looked at as one big secretive undertaking. The three picturesque picnic structures in the park, with varying amounts of massive peeled log and stone were named after famous Sioux leaders. The Sioux were only one of many tribes that once inhabited the area of East Central Wyoming, but names from this tribe were well known across American.

In the 1930s the Wild West and Wild West themes and names were popular throughout America. It is most probable the names of the Indian Chiefs used in the park were chosen because they were notable in history and the names would be easy to remember.

The three Indian leaders came from different bands of the Lakota. Different bands, but they were all Sioux and at the time of the Indian wars, contemporaries. The Indian Wars were an important time in history along the trails that followed the North Platte River of Eastern Wyoming.

Fort Laramie

Fort Laramie, only fifteen miles from the park entrance, was a hotbed of activity during that time in American Western History. The fort is a popular tourist site and a place that makes for a great day trip for campers at Guernsey State Park.

Parade Grounds at Fort Laramie

Spotted Tail was a leader during the Grattan Massacre, one of the most written about skirmishes involving soldiers from Fort Laramie. The Grattan site is well marked and located a few miles east of the fort. Historically the 1854 Grattan Massacre is often thought to be the start of the Indian Wars in the west.[12]

Red Cloud and Sitting Bull were most active during the series of battles referred to as, Red Cloud's War. For a few years the soldiers of Fort Laramie had the impossible task of trying to protect travelers heading west on the Oregon and Mormon Trails and North to the gold fields on the Bozeman.

Sitting Bull Shelter

Nothing is recorded as to why the use of Native Indian leader's names in the park stopped with these three structures, but nowhere else in the park is anything named after Native people.

Sitting Bull, Red Cloud and Spotted Tail along with Gaul and Crazy Horse are probably the most well know Indian leaders in the west.

Red Cloud was best known for his war against people traveling the Bozeman Trail. He also fought against the forts protecting the trail. After a disastrous defeat at the Wagon Box Fight, near Fort Phil Kearny, Red Cloud turned his efforts to peace. His peace efforts made him most popular with settlers and travelers, along with some of his tribe, but these efforts also alienated him from some of his people.[13]

Sitting Bull was a Lakota Holy Man and respected leader, most forceful during the time of Crazy Horse. Sitting Bull, although he did not take part in the massacre, was instrumental when Colonel Custer and the 7th Calvary were wiped out on the Greasy Grass River, the river the soldiers called the Little Big Horn. Later Sitting Bull traveled to Europe with Buffalo Bill's Wild West Show. He was murdered at Wounded Knee South Dakota shortly before the December 1890 massacre.[14]

Spotted Tail seems an odd choice for the third Indian name used in the park. Considering fame only, it seems Crazy Horse would have been the choice instead of Spotted Tail. He was likely chosen because he had taken part in the nearby Grattan Massacre. By the time of Red Cloud's War Spotted Tail refused to fight, telling his people he would not lead braves into battle and that he now considered peace the better option.[15] Conceivably it was because of this peaceful stance and not his earlier status as a warrior that he was chosen to be immortalized in the park.

There are no longer Bison in the Park, although they were tried as an experiment in the 1980s.

Much of the area around Guernsey State Park and along the North Platte River was prime Buffalo country. The short hard grass, plentiful water and lack of heavy winter snows made the area perfect for survival of both native peoples and the bison. This combination of weather and a plentiful supply of meat and water made the wandering, hunting lifestyle possible for the last of the Plains Indian tribes.

Powderhouse

Near a sharp bend in the road, a mile north of the three picnic shelters stands one of four small earth sheltered Civilian Conservation Corps work crew powderhouses in the park.

Powderhouse on Lakeshore Drive

These small rock buildings were used to store explosives for workers dynamiting their way along what would become Lakeshore Drive. This limestone and packed earth dugout style building is only a few feet off the road. There is an interpretive sign and a place to park a few feet north of the powderhouse. This structure is the Dead Man's Gulch Powderhouse, now there is a name for the ages!

Lakeshore Bridges

This stretch of Lakeshore drive is also the site of one of two CCC bridges in the park. The two bridges are less than a mile apart and are the only Civilian Conservation Corps road bridges in the park. Like other building structures in Guernsey State Park the bridges are predominately of layered limestone blocks and peeled log construction. In more recent times the bridge decking has been rebuilt to support the added weight of asphalt paving that has for many years replaced the original gravel once topping Lakeshore Drive.

The two bridges were built predominately to handle spring run-off, and intermittent creek water as there are no, fulltime, live water streams in the area.

Lakeshore Drive Bridge near Fish Canyon

The Cap House and a Second Powderhouse

A few yards after crossing the bridge there is a path leading north through the trees into a mountain park open area. Approximatively sixty yards off the Drive, and out of site from the road are two more powderhouses.

The first is approximately the same size as the more visible one sitting a few yards east of Lakeshore Drive. It is marked with the same interpretive sign as the previous shelter. This shelter has the roughhewn wood door propped open affording a view of the inside structure. A warning here, the cool of the inside of this type of building would make an excellent resting place for a rattlesnake on a hot summer day. Don't let that worry you, but please, be cautious when peeking inside.

The Second Powderhouse at Dead Man's Gulch

Of more significance to history buffs may be the small cap-house where dynamite caps were stored away from the main explosives.

The Cap House

The cap-house is a dollhouse-like version of the parks three larger powderhouses. The inside of the cap house shows flat stone walls, stone floor and ceiling with a wood frame in the front to attach a door. The entirety of the inside is only about three feet deep and two feet wide, but it served its purpose.

The Cap House is located about 100 yards north and slightly east of the larger Powderhouse.

The three powderhouses, grouped together on Lakeshore Drive, give visitors an idea of how much dynamite and blasting was required as the Civilian Conservation Corps crews built the road. The original road was built sixteen feet wide and expanded a few feet in critical places. The modern day road is wider but remains the originally designed and constructed drive.

A Black Bear in the Park

Although sightings are rare, often years between, visitors as recently as the summer of 2013 have sighted Black Bears in the park. They are wary and mostly nocturnal creatures and the likelihood of seeing one are next to zero – but they are around.

Bear Scat – Spring, 2014

Dead Man's Gulch

Looking East up Dead Man's Gulch

Some places in the park appear to have went through name changes after completion of construction. Names of roads, buildings and areas of interest are often based on someone famous, a politician or an interesting story. In the case of naming Dead Man's Gulch, it is a most interesting story, fascinating and a bit macabre. The story of Dead Man's Gulch sounds more like a tale out of a mining camp or a startup rough and tumble old-west town, but in this case, it's a story about a ditch, Westerners call them gulches, this one is just off a bend in the road built by the CCC. More than a decade before the turn of the twentieth century, likely the mid-1880s, a body was discovered in a gulch along what would someday become Guernsey

State Park's stunning, Lakeshore Drive. The gulch itself splits and the body was described as being a ways up the right hand ditch. When found, the remains had been decomposing so long it was impossible to identify. The only remarkable thing about the body was a pair of spurs with solid silver rowels, a few shredded pieces of cloth were found where the clothes should have been. What was left of the body had long since become but a small pile of bones. Years of decomposition had claimed the rest.

In a climate as dry as Guernsey's it would have taken more than a decade, possibly several, to reach the stage of decomposition of the body found in the gulch.

No sign of a weapon, saddle or a horse were left behind. He must have been on horseback, but even that is only a guess, an educated guess, because he wore spurs. So, who was this unknown man with the fancy spurs? Was he a cowboy, a trapper, a mountain man, soldier, or possibly a deserter from nearby Fort Laramie? Perhaps he was only an everyday drifter? Possibly he was running from the law, wounded, like in old western movies. Maybe it wasn't a man at all could it have been a women? Many stories, with slight variations have been told of the dead man in the gulch. To add to the mystery, no name was recorded as to who found the decomposed body. The greatest part of the mystery remains, what happened to the spurs with the silver rowels?

My personal favorite story goes something like this.

The Story of the Body in the Gulch

A man, known only as Black, nobody really knew if Black was his last name or a nickname. He had been in and around the Cheyenne to Black Hills stage route for several weeks, sometimes riding shotgun on one of the dangerous runs. More often, if he had money, he hung around the Cheyenne Club or one of the many gambling concerns in Deadwood.

Once when a stage traveler admired his fancy spurs he said he'd won them in a poker game. Another time he mentioned buying them in Mexico.

Curious people questioned how someone who apparently did not work on a regular basis could afford such an expensive pair of spurs. But why not, he was also described as wearing handmade boots he'd special ordered to fit his feet. Some of the new style, individually made from a place in Kansas.

Privately Black had told a table of his poker playing pals that he found the spurs on a body, "a way's up a gulch," near the North Platte River. Since he was more often broke than not most believed this to be true. So how does all of this tie into a story?

The real story might be the finding of the body, one man found it, no one else ever saw it. The man, Black, who proudly owned a new set of spurs appeared only briefly in the area and never was heard from again. A few years' later locals commonly believed that no one simply walked upon a decaying body with the spurs. Instead believing someone was killed in the gulch, most stories named Black as the killer, with the spurs being part, or all of the take from the crime.

Some modern tales make the dead man out as a park haunting ghost who today frequents the Red Cloud shelter area. But who was he really? The man might have been a murderer lawman with the body later dumped in the gulch or a drummer (traveling peddler), or a women. Today when the wind blows out of the south-south-west an eerie, haunting howl, can be heard in and around Dead Man's Gulch. The entirety of the story sounds much more like a tall-tale than history, and perhaps it is, but the story of the Dead Man's Gulch still makes for lively conversation more than a century later. [16]

The Dead Man in the Gulch?

Storytellers can add in a few spicy details, these can be made up on the spot, include a handful of scary fine points, and what better ghost story to tell while setting around a roaring late evening campfire in the Red Cloud picnic area? Toss in a belly full of fire roasted marshmallows and you have the perfect summer evening story at Guernsey State Park.

Rock Climbing in the Park

Occasionally unexpected things happen in areas of the park that surprise even long time visitors. At Dead Man's Gulch an unforeseen use has become one of the most intriguing and attention grabbing park activities. For years only a handful of hikers and photographers frequented this area of the park which now has become a popular rock climbing site.

According to the *Mountain Project's* rock climbing web page this popular climb is on a wall they have christened, "The Revolutionary Climbing Wall."[17]

The Revolutionary climb is up a large south facing red sedimentary rock wall. This rock is located near the area where the gulch splits. Today we can be sure the planners from the Civilian Conservation Corps never thought about this one.

The Revolutionary Climbing wall at Dead Man's Gulch

Lakeshore Drive

The work on the parks east side Lakeshore Drive, included numerous culverts, bridges and walls. Most of this rock work is still in use and as good today as when it was built eighty years ago. Building the scenic drive called for much blasting and even more pick and shovel handwork. CCC diaries relate stories of workers early in the program who did not want to work that hard.

Lakeshore Drive – Photo from the Castle

For the few workers who believed the job was some kind of government handout, they didn't last long.[18] The workers who stuck around became hard workers, most of them taking tremendous pride in what they were building in the new Guernsey Lake State Park.

Mysteries of the Park

Most anything more than three quarters of a century old and encompassing thousands of acres with mountains, forest lands and water must hold some mysteries. Guernsey State Park is no exception, and the mysterious man at Dead Man's Gulch is only one of many great tales the park holds.

East Side Park Mysteries

Guernsey State Park is rich in both history and folklore. The park has had its share of unusual happenings, oddities and strange stories. This work takes a quick look at two mysteries on each side of the lake. The men of the CCC were constantly looking for something to start a conversation. What better than a great, east side of the lake mystery?

The Onyx Cave and Onyx Cave Trail

A trail that at one time was to be the focus of the park trails system today qualifies as a first rate mystery of the park. On the east side the abandoned Onyx Cave and the long forgotten Onyx Cave Trail or road is nearly unknown by present day visitors. An early CCC map, when work was being started at the camp, shows the Onyx Cave Trail and no other trails on the east side. When the east side trail system was in the building stage the Onyx Cave Trail was to become the centerpiece of the east side trails system.[19]

By the second phase of trail building the trail no longer appeared on Bureau of Reclamation park maps.[20] Today the trail shows up on no park maps, but it can be found by careful searchers. The trail head is in the Upper Spotted Tail Campground. The trail starts a bit east of the restrooms and follows the hillside for about a quarter of a mile then dips down and crosses a dry wash. After scrambling up out of the dry creek the hiker will be on a well-marked, from use, old road. The trail, actually the old Onyx Cave Road is an easy walk for experienced hikers and not bad for casual walkers.

There is also a trail head about one hundred yards north of the Upper Spotted Tail Campground, on the east side of the road. The entrance is blocked by two large cut boulders. This road leads one-hundred and fifty yards to a Y, the left branch going north to a private cabin, the right hand branch becomes the trail to the Onyx Mine. Vehicles are not allowed on the trail but it is an easy walk along a well-marked trail.

The old road winds up to the mine. I am not sure why it was so often referred to as a cave instead of the mine it was. I have found no evidence it was ever a natural cave later developed into a mine, but this might be a sensible assumption. Or the word cave may have been a local colloquialism for a mine. The mine, long since closed, has its entrance caved in, permanently shut to rock hounds and curiosity seekers alike. A thorough search of the area can still yield many small pieces of Onyx. The cave is only a few feet off the trail, broken boulders and rock pieces make it easy to find.

Onyx Road/Trail to the Cave

Onyx Quarry Site

In 1893 a large block of Onyx from this mine or a sister onyx mine boarding the parks north boundary, was polished and shipped to the Chicago World's Fair. That prize piece now rests beside the flagpole in nearby Hartville's, Boot Hill Cemetery. The area of the Onyx Cave is strewn with limestone boulders, many of them cut but never used.

What was 3122 Co. Road?

One huge boulder, near the mine is carved with, 3122 CO. ROAD, but I have been unable to come up with any information as to what company the road was built for, what the 3122 might mean, or anything else for that matter.

3122 CO. ROAD Rock

It is possible the CCC cut some rock here as well as in the east side quarry. It is also possible the limestone was cut along with Onyx at the site. Rock may have also been cut from here for other area projects. The way the limestone was drilled and cut might indicate it was cut by miners knowledgeable of splitting rock. Possibly it was used for projects at the Sunrise Iron Ore mine only a few miles away.

Drilled and Split Limestone

It is feasible that no one will ever find out the significance of the carved rock reading, "3122 CO. ROAD," but speculation remains that it had something to do with the Civilian Conservation Corps and not the Onyx Mine or the Sunrise Mine a few miles away. Suggestions from local historians speculate it could have had something to do with Fort Laramie. Sometimes the best mysteries are real and not fiction.

Once the trail passes the Onyx Cave the path wanders up a rather steep hill to a fence line. This fence marks the end of state park property. The trail here turns ninety degrees right, south, and leads a quarter mile to the old golf course. The old trail circled the golf course and ended at the Museum. Today an unfortunate vehicle trail crosses what was once the fourth and eight fairways of Camp BR-9 Links at Guernsey Lake, Golf Course. This rutted two-track leads southwest through the old parking lot and eventually follows, what's left of, the old golf course road leading west until it meets the Museum road.

Hikers walking to the old mine should be aware it is only about a third of the distance to walk in from the Spotted Tail entrance and to walk back out the same way. The walk from Spotted Tail around the mine, golf course and Museum, is three, or so, miles long, but on a warm summer day, quite rewarding. A note for those taking the hike, there is a drinking fountain and restrooms available at the Museum.

A Second Mystery from the Park's East Side

A second mystery from the parks east side reads somewhat like the playing-cards from the game of "Clue." That mystery is the lost treasure or the lost hidden loot of legendary bad man Jake Slade.

Jake Slade's hidden (stolen) Treasure

Jake Slade

We know, at least according to legend, it was a man named Jake Slade who robbed gold from Overland Stage Coaches, so we know who and what. What we do not know is where he hid it. Adventurous treasure hunters have combed the hills and canyons of the park and nearby areas for more than a century looking for Jack Slade's hidden gold. Thus the mystery of the Guernsey Lake State Park lost treasure was born.

The story of Slade's buried treasure of gold was often described as up to thirty different caches buried in the area. No doubt some of the men of camp BR-9 heard the stories. Maybe some of these adventurous young men used their week-end free time to tramp towards Sawmill Canyon in hopes of getting rich. It would have been much more than the $30 a month they were making.

Jack Slade was a popular or unpopular, depending on the source, stationmaster on the Overland Stage Route. Those who knew him well liked him when he was sober, but hated who he became when he was drinking, and at times that was all-too often. Although the station he superintended was 130 miles away, south of Laramie, the Slade Gang kept a hideout in Sawmill Canyon, two miles north and west of the park. To reach the hideout they rode through the northern part of what today is Guernsey State Park. Some treasure hunters, thinking him a practical outlaw, believe he may have stashed some of the loot before he rode the last few miles into Sawmill Canyon where the rest of the gang waited for their leader. Stashed the gold in the park, who knows?[21]

How famous was Jake Slade? Mark Twain met him, and wrote about him in his famous going west book, *Roughing It*.[22] Seems like he didn't care much for Slade, this is what he had to say.

"A high and efficient servant of the Overland, an outlaw among outlaws and yet their relentless scourge, Slade was at once the most bloody, the most dangerous and the most valuable citizen that inhabited the savage fastnesses of the mountains." [23]

Looking North into Slade Country

Slade was referred to as a conscientious employee of the stage company by some who knew him. Others called him a ruthless murdering outlaw. So which person was he, the outlaw or the hardworking employee? History may never know which man he really was, but what we do know is, Jake Slade created one of this state parks and one of America's greatest hidden treasure mysteries, the Slade gang's hidden gold.

Maybe it's still there for the finding, treasure hunters are still looking.

There are many Canyon and Mountain Sites throughout the Park where Slade may have hidden the Gold

The Museum

Undeniably the most impressive structure in the park is the huge limestone block and wood timber Museum. Built by Camp BR-9, the first CCC camp in the park, construction took longer than the building of any other single Civilian Conservation Corps project in the park. 6,100 man hours were needed to complete the Museum.[24] In 1933 the National Park Service sent a park planner and an architect, Conrad Wirth and Thomas Vint to see the new Bureau of Reclamation Lake in Guernsey Wyoming.[25]

The two would set about the task of planning the buildings and recreation areas for everything on the east side of the lake. The Museum stands as a monument to the long-lasting effect the two had on Guernsey State Park.

Building Front Archway of Museum

Photo - Wyoming State Archives, Department of State Parks and Cultural Resources

This brilliant piece of prairie architecture is a one of a kind limestone and log structure. Like the North Bluff Castle, and the shelter at Sitting Bull, the Museum was built in the style of the new Rustic Architecture movement of the National Park Service. The National Park Service used this architectural style on nearly everything they built during the middle of the twentieth century. Yellowstone National Park is packed with fine examples of Rustic Architectural buildings. The Park Service used this style so often that it was sometimes referred to as Parkitecture.[26] Of all the state parks in Wyoming only Guernsey State Park became part of the, now long forgotten, Parkitecture movement.

Museum Parkitecture Inspectors
Photo - Wyoming State Archives, Department of State Parks and Cultural Resources

The Museum is one of the finest examples in America of this nonintrusive building style, blending buildings into nature. Parts of the Museum seem to rise up from the ground instead of being built on the ground. This look was the goal. Both the Museum and the shelter at Sitting Bull seem to accomplish this objective quite well.

The completed Museum is 59 X 101 feet. The original displays are nearly untouched since they were built in 1937 as innovative, top of the line exhibits.

The floor of the Museum was quarried, cut numbered and assembled in Thermopolis, Wyoming, then torn apart, packed and shipped to Guernsey to be reassembled in the Museum. Nearly 80 years later a few numbers are still visible on the floor in the south wing, near the buildings southern and western walls.

Museum Displays

Intricately cut, numbered, and placed Museum floor

The Museum was built nearly handicap assessable, rather unusual for the time. Only a single step up gets visitors to the Museum floor level, today a small ramp makes it quite Handicap usable.

Women's Restroom at the Museum

The original accessibility may have had more to do with the architecture of the building than any thoughts of ease of entry. But the huge front door and no step entry on the south side make it as ADA compliant today as many modern buildings.

Although the Museum has an upper parking lot that will accommodate several cars, it was built with a lower area parking lot with steps to reach the Museum. The steps are another fine example of rustic use of native stone laid so that they seem to blend into and become part of the hillside.

One of Two Sets of Steps from the Lower Lot to the Museum

Today the Museum is essentially the same as when finished by the CCC. Inside are two large exhibit halls and a cozy library dominated by a large fireplace. The two halls hold 14 specially made display cases depicting the history and prehistory of the surrounding area. The Museum and displays allow visitors a view of the Guernsey State Park area long before settlement came to the area. The Museum and the display cases inside are in and of themselves a great lesson in Civilian Conservation Corps history, ingenuity, building and forethought.

Museum South Wing

Over the years, new roofs, plumbing work and some electrical updates have dominated the upkeep of the Museum. A new furnace and an updated sewer system have been the most recent upgrades. Be assured when one steps into the Museum it is virtually the same as it was when completed in 1936 with no changes in the basic blueprint, look or feel of the building.

The Museum grounds are also the starting point for two well used and enjoyable east side, CCC built walking trails.

The Museum Setting in Front of Round Top Mountain
A Rustic Blend of Nature and Building

Additional East Side Projects

Not all Camp BR-9 workers spent their days building the Museum. Many projects were completed while building of the Museum was in progress and much work on the east side of the park was finished in the two years after the Museum was built. When the work on the east side was complete there were 22 buildings, several miles of roads along with numerous rock retaining walls, culverts, rock lined drainage areas, trail steps, several miles of walking trails, a golf course, tennis court, fire pits, and picnic tables along with newly planted trees and shrubs.

Stone Culvert on Lakeshore Drive

But what the government gives they can also take away and they did. Shortly after the closure of Camp BR-9 the Army moved the large recreation hall, (20x84) and one of the barracks to camp BR-83 in Veteran, Wyoming. A few months' later two more of the barracks were partly disassembled and moved to Camp BR-1 in Minatare, Nebraska.[27] Some buildings, such as the Education Building, were left for a while longer, but eventually all but two were torn down or moved to other CCC camps.

Education Building at Camp BR-9
Photo - Wyoming State Archives, Department of State Parks and Cultural Resources

Chapter 3 – The West Side

Camp BR-10

On July 6, 1934 a second CCC camp was opened at Guernsey Lake State Park.[28] A scant six weeks after the opening of BR-9 on the east side, Camp DBR-10 opened on the west side. This second camp would initially be occupied by the men of Company No. 1858. The camp, set in a flat park like valley, was located a mile west of the dam. The D in DBR identified the camp as a drought relief camp.

Drought relief camps were located, throughout the American West, in states recognized as suffering from severe drought. The work and pay for the laboring men of the Civilian Conservation Corps was the same as in any other classification of camp, but the funding came from a different area of government appropriations. The camp did not last long as a drought relief camp as it was shortly reclassified a Bureau of Reclamation Camp and became Guernsey Lake Camp BR-10.

Like Camp BR-9, BR-10 was first charged with building a road for tourists and recreationists. On the east side, Lakeshore Drive was replicated with a road on the west side, soon to be named Skyline Drive. Unlike the east side camp, the west side camp would be short lived. BR-10 would operate for only 18 months, but in the short year and a half span much impressive work was completed and other projects were well underway when the men of BR-10 were moved out.

Herd of Mule Deer on Skyline Drive north of Camp BR-10

Skyline Drive

What would soon become Skyline Drive turned west well before the dam and wound its way to a terminating beautiful overlook referred to as the North-Bluff. Skyline Drive today follows the original road turning west at the park entry pay station. Along the road the men of Camp BR-10 built trails, pull-off viewing areas, campsites, picnic areas and restrooms, referred to as comfort stations in early CCC documents. The culminating turn-around on Skyline Drive at the North Bluff features the wonderful and popular Guernsey State Park Castle and the Million Dollar Biffy.

North Bluff Castle – Southwest View

It should be noted here that of all the work completed on the west side, none of the Sandy Beach area is CCC work. Maps show no roads or work in this area. The work on the west side was done east of Skyline Drive, between the road and the lake. Some cleaning and grooming was done on an area called, Bathing Beach, at Davis Bay, leading some to conclude, the CCC built the Sandy Beach swimming, camping and boat dock area. But today's popular Sandy Beach was not built by the CCC. Bathing Beach, was a generic map term referring to the east side boat dock area, cleaned and groomed as a beach by BR-9.

Early plans called for adding a bath house on each side and cleanup of double the five acres of beach that had been finished, but time ran out before this part of the plan was started. The swimming beach with a modern bath house on the west side was left on the drawing board and to imagination along with a bathhouse and additional beach area on the east side of the park.

Davis Bay

Constantly changing water levels likely caused the CCC to back off from some of these ideas. Sandy Beach, many years later, would better fit the ever changing reservoir levels. There is still a small beach area at Davis Bay, not much used by swimmers but it still remains popular as a sun bathing and wading area.

Mae West Hill

Skyline Drive, itself, was to be the featured attraction on the west side, with trails, hiking and narrow driving roads leading from the main drive to places of interest and importance. Shortly after turning west off Skyline Drive the first major obstacle of road building faced the men.

A small mountain, one the men soon called, Mae West Hill, would be a steep and dangerous engineering and building project.

The name Mae West Hill was at first an inside joke for the workers and supervisors. The men felt something with this many ups and downs and so many curves needed a fitting name. Movie star Mae West seemed to have plenty of curves and that is how her name became attached to a small mountain in Guernsey State Park, complements of the working men of the CCC. It doesn't appear any modern day maps use the name Mae West Hill but several maps and photos do label it, as such, throughout the phases of building the Park.[29]

Today many locals still refer to Mae West Hill, younger generations and park newbies might look at someone using the name with some amount of puzzlement. People using the term, Mae West Hill today are either, park experts or long time visitors.

**Summer 2014 Super Moon Rises
Over
Mae West Hill**

The Site for Camp BR-10

At the west side bottom of Mae West Hill, on the south side of the road, sat Camp BR-10 of the Civilian Conservation Corps. The camp had a short life of only a year and a half but the setting in the west side park mountain valley was most extraordinary.

Camp BR-10
Photo Wyoming State Archives, Department of State Parks and Cultural Resources

One mile after Skyline Drive passes the site of Camp Br-10, the road crosses a very nice rock walled railroad bridge. From a distance the bridge looks like a flat board lying between two hills. For decades this bridge was a tunnel hiding trains along the way but now it affords a nice view of trains rolling through the parks southernmost boundary.

Train traveling toward the Park Bridge

Newell Bay

Immediately after crossing the bridge a gravel road leads east to Newell Bay, the first of two large bays on the west side. Another half mile north reaches the drive to Brimmer Point and after another quarter of a mile north the road to Davis Bay. These three areas are well used today. The two bays are popular camping, picnicking, hiking, and sightseeing areas.

Newell Bay, referred to in early CCC materials with several citations including, the Bay, regatta area or simply picnic area."[30] This bay area includes two areas which Y off the road today called

Newell Bay Road. To the right the Y leads to a prominent peninsula with tables and restrooms for picnickers and sightseers.

Newell Bay

If any CCC work remains at Newell Bay, other than the trail road and some landscaping it is hard to find. Possibly parts of the two sets of crumbling steps leading down a steep embankment to the water, were CCC built but any reference to step work here could not be found. The steps, made of concrete, are recognizably post CCC, indeed the north steps have '81' scratched into the lowest one. Possibly they replaced CCC steps, if they do, any signs of the original steps have long since been reclaimed by nature and the rising and falling water levels of the lake.

Steps at Newell Bay

The left hand road off the Y leads to a developed cabin area, the only cabin area on the west side. This area sits atop a high knob with great views of the lake along with the hills and mountains surrounding the park. There is also a small picnic spot in the area.

Another point of interest about Newell Bay is that some early maps label it as Holdring Bay and several label it as the regatta area. This area parallels the peninsula that is a day use area today. It is prominently labeled on several of the Bureau of Reclamation CCC maps.[31] I am not sure if any type of racing regatta was ever held in this area but it would have been the perfect setting. The side hills of this peninsula offered stadium like seating for spectators watching the races in Newell Bay below.

This area remains one of the unique spots in and around the park. A place where visitors can still close their eyes and imagine what it was like long ago. And maybe, just maybe, if you hold yours eyes, shut tight, and hold them long enough, a real dreamer might be able to see small sail boats and crew racing boats with spectators above cheering them on. Sadly the idea of Sunday afternoons in the summer sun watching a regatta likely died a death of the times.

Brimmer Point

Brimmer Point and the road leading to this, highest point in the park, were intended to be one of the highlights of Skyline Drive. The Point, setting at the top of Powell Mountain is named after an influential Cheyenne businessman who helped push legislation to build the park. Brimmer Point features a prairie style sandstone viewing area. Built up twenty feet above the parking lot the viewing level is reached by a beautifully made set of curving stone steps leading to the observation platform. The Civilian Conservation Corps built steps and the viewing area blend into the landscape almost unnoticed to the casual observer.

The Point

    Roughly half way to Brimmer Point in a deep valley before the final climb up Powell mountain are two trail heads with a beautiful stone and peeled timber bridge to start the walk. The bridge is one of two walk bridges in the park, the other is located on the Tunnel Mountain Trail. These bridges were built by BR-10, in an elaborate style, rivaling the road bridges on the east side of the park.

    Unfortunately the timbers of both bridges were destroyed in the devastating fire of 2012 and have not yet (as of summer 2014), been scheduled for reconstruction. These bridges are such a great piece of Civilian Conservation Corps history that rebuilding is an absolute necessity to the integrity of the parks trail system and to the wonderful history of the CCC in the park.

Walk Bridge on Brimmer Point Trail, before the Fire

The road to Brimmer Point is a marvel of engineering itself. Climbing and winding up Powell Mountain and at one point curving down through a deep valley. It is a slow but breathtaking drive. In places the drive can be heart thumping with views straight down the side of the mountain. The road and drive are not dangerous but the prudent driver will keep to a slow 15 to 20 mph most of the way. Brimmer Point setting atop Powell Mountain, the highest point in the park, can be seen for miles. The work of the CCC in building the point was a marvel of both CCC engineering and just plain hard work and courage of the young men involved.

Brimmer Point – Lake View

It must have taken a certain kind of brave individual to work on top of this mountain. In places the chain link fence is mere inches away from sheer cliffs hundreds of feet above the lake or lakeshore below.

Two most innovative construction techniques were used on Brimmer Point. The chain-link fencing holding back sight seers from the sheer cliff drop-offs was one of the first uses of this new type of fencing in an American park. The fence, now eighty years old, still looks as good as new. The chain-link was manufactured, marked and shipped to Guernsey under of the authority of the National Park Service. In places the markings on the fence are still legible.

Painted Label on Fence from the 1930s

It appears that the rails and posts were labeled sequentially to make putting the fence up easier. The fence was built with handmade hold downs, designed and forged by the workers and screw-anchored into solid rock.

Hand Forged - Hold-Downs

The Point can be seen from most of the east side of the park and many west side areas along Skyline Drive. Many who climb the overlook do not take the time to look west, but the view toward Laramie peak is as spectacular as the eastern view of the lake. Brimmer Point can be spotted from several places around the area and from nearby Guernsey. The view of the Point from the eighth tee at Trail Ruts Golf Course, south of Guernsey, is magnificent.

Brimmer Point view from the Museum

Davis Bay

An area listed on the earliest CCC maps as Ledbetter Canyon, but long sense referred to as Davis Bay, is a small underutilized camping and hiking area. The hiking trails lead both south, the Davis Bay to Brimmer Point Trail, and north on Lakeview Trail. The improvements at Davis Bay were built with day users in mind. A chance for both locals and vacationers alike to get in the water on a hot summer day. In early park times it was a popular row-boating, picnicking and hiking area but those uses have dwindled to almost nothing in modern times. Original maps also show a developed beach area at the Bay and plans for a possible combination beach house and dressing facility but construction was never started.[32] Today modern restrooms and a handful of nice camping spots are the featured attractions for the area.

CCC work in the Davis Bay area include a set of large stone steps, now unused, on a trail no longer marked, nor can it be easily found. In the case of this trail it is possible it was never finished. The CCC often built steps first with the trail to come later.

Steps to Nowhere

It is probable that Camp BR-10 was decommissioned before the trail could be built, leaving a set of stone steps to nowhere. These steps can be found by following the east trail from Davis Bay. They are down the trail only a quarter of a mile and on the left, or north side of the trail. Interesting to speculate.

Echo Cave

Camp BR-10 men built steep steps and a short rugged trail to a small cavern in the wall high above the lake. Echo Cave, once a popular place for kids of all ages to yell at the top of their lungs for the familiar echo.

Visitors have marked the Cave over the Years

The men building this area may have been the first to find the echo and likely annoyed the boss with their, every once in a while, yell for the return of the echo. The trail and the cave, not far from the North Bluff Castle, were still marked a few years ago, but the deteriorating condition of the area along parts of the trail makes a trip to Echo Cave somewhat less safe than it once was. Signs were removed years ago and park maps no longer list Echo Cave or the trail to it.

Echo Cave Trail

The cave was a well-used and much loved part of the park for many years; unfortunately today, because of safety issues, it is mostly remembered through the reminiscences of people from decades past.

The trail is unmarked but not blocked-off and can still be negotiated by people who are careful. Park staff continues to maintain the trail, cleaning the steps and brush from the walking path. Generations of kids from Platte County grew up shouting from Echo Cave and listening to the music of the prominent echo.

The View from Echo Cave

Today if someone wants to hear the famous Guernsey State Park echo, this writer, along with his six grandchildren, have found the fence on the cliff behind the Castle is a safer and more than satisfactory substitution as an echo area. And if you have the kids or grandkids along, it is as much fun as when we were kids, give it a long and loud holler then listen for the prominent echo.

Echo Cave – Photo taken from Lakeshore Drive across the lake

Skyline Drive Pull-Offs

Alert travelers on Skyline Drive may spot the remains of several, CCC built, vehicle pull-offs, now out of use for decades. These site are along the east side of the road, at various locations along the Drive, affording picturesque views and photo opportunities of the lake.

The pull-offs, although popular many years ago are much too small for today's larger vehicles and campers that frequent the park. In most cases these areas would have accommodated only one or two modern vehicles, making upkeep too expensive.

View of the Lake from a Pull-Off on Skyline Drive

The CCC Rock Quarry

The remains of the Civilian Conservation Corps quarry, used to mine stone for work throughout the park, is also located on the west side a mile south of the castle. The quarry can be reached by visitors on bikes, and hikers who wish to walk past on nearby trails.

The quarry is overgrown and much of the exposed limestone is crumbled and weathered, removing most of the sign of quarrying on the walls. Some large, usable looking, rock slabs are lying above and in the quarry.

The road leading in and out of the quarry is still visible but is marked, *authorized vehicles only.* For CCC history buffs a hike or bicycle ride on nearby trails to the old quarry is a must. The quarry is not on park maps and not easily accessible, keeping historians and curiosity seekers at bay. Too bad, because it is likely one of only a few, if in fact there are any, untouched and never reclaimed CCC work sights remaining.

CCC Quarry

The West Side Trail System

The trailhead for the west side of the park lies on the intersection of Skyline Drive and Brimmer Point Road. From that juncture many of the original CCC trails of varying amounts of difficulty can be walked, hiked or traveled by trail bikes.

The trails today are much used, but like many parts of the park where the CCC had hopes and plans for more than was completed, the dreamed of extra miles of trails were cut. A nice interpretive sign explains the trails to anyone who might be in the mood for some exercise.

Trails are still marked, in present day, with original or reproductions of the original log markers. The first built trails were marked with simple painted signs but as the men had time new log markers were made at the east side Camp-9 shop.

Trail Sign and Map at Intersection

Building of the trails was a priority of the CCC workers as they were meant to be the recreational focus of the park. The west side, less developed and rougher than the east, had trails built featuring outstanding views of the lake and of the mountains surrounding the park.

Log Trail Marker in the Park

The North Bluff Castle

At the end of Skyline Drive is the most impressive piece of Civilian Conservation Corps work on the west side. The North Bluff Castle, interestingly referred to in CCC documents as the North Bluff Picnic Shelter, the name was yet to come.[33]

This North Bluff Shelter is built along the lines of the Rustic Architecture Movement but with a bit more of a Spanish influence and a Southwestern feel.

The North Bluff Castle

The Castle may be the most spectacular picnic shelter in the United States, with its enormous log supports, limestone rock walls and the massive fireplace, it stands alone as a most unique structure. The Castle, with its distinctive peeled logs tied together with the stonework is, like the Museum on the east side, a park showpiece. The Castle has become one of the most photographed buildings in the Wyoming State Park System. Taking a photo of the castle when vacationing in Eastern Wyoming has become a parallel to a photo of old Faithful Lodge when in Yellowstone. The Castle is so well know that it has been written about in publications as far away as Australia.

In *Boles Blogs*,[34] one of Australia's most popular blogs, followed and read by thousands, Ken

Druce wrote. "I took a last trip up to the Castle just before I moved to Australia. There are a few areas I knew I would miss, but none as much as Lake Guernsey. I spent the afternoon and took some pictures as a physical remembrance. I doubt I shall ever go there again. That makes me sad, but also happy, since I have such a peaceful place to go back to in my dreams and memories. Whenever the world gets me down, I just let go and feel myself being lifted up and taken to my place of peace. A kingdom of one, contentedly."[35]

Two unique features set the Castle apart from most other picnic shelters in America. The first is the winding spiral staircase leading to an overlook atop the Castle. The flat sandstone steps were carefully cut and fitted by hand, fit so precisely they almost feel natural, as if they were steps up the side of a mountain put in place by nature.

The overlook affords one of the best views of the park and the North Platte River country in America. On a clear day the view to the west makes Laramie Peak seem only an arm's reach away.

Looking west toward Laramie Peak from the Castle

The Castle, made up of two massive rooms, each with an impressive stone archways a second most extraordinary feature of this shelter. Standing next to the fireplace it is easy to see the time consuming workmanship in the finely fit stone and log of the building. Looking west through the two inside arches, Laramie Peak, is framed most impressively. It took much planning and some fine building skills to get it just right.

Great pride was taken with the laying of each stone and the pacing of each timber, the CCC workers of Camp BR-10 and later BR-9, knew this structure would be the crowning jewel of their construction projects on the west side of the park and thousands of visitors each year will agree that they got it perfect.

Laramie Peak framed through the Castle Arches

Million Dollar Biffy

The illustrious Biffy

Eighty yards south of the Castle stands the Million Dollar Biffy, this is the most impressive restroom/outhouse, perhaps anywhere. Like the Castle it is of massive stone and peeled timber construction. Referred to in BR-10 notes as the North Bluff comfort station, it stands alone as the greatest symbol of the competition between the craftsmen of Guernsey CCC camps BR-9 and BR-10.

This restroom, built of brown and buff sandstone, at a cost of $6,000 might cost closer to the million it's named after if it were to be rebuilt today. One can only wonder today if the builders thought someone was out of their mind when they drew the plans for this restroom. Or did these young workers smile, laugh and shake their heads, every day they went to work on the Million Dollar Biffy.

West Side Park Mysteries

Mysteries abound throughout the park and two strange places on the west side fit into the cozy mystery arena. The first qualifying place is the chimney and remains of a small foundation on a point overlooking Davis Bay. The old cabin ruins set amidst pines and cedars, with a fine view of the river and lake another one hundred yards to the east. If the cabin was still in use after the lake was built, it sat on the south side of the bay about half way between land and the water. The area can be reached by a walking path and stands about 150 yards from the cable fence marking the end of the Davis Bay camping and day use areas.

Only the Fireplace still stands from the Mysterious Old Cabin

Who lived there, when did he leave, what did he/she do? One early map of the area is marked with the word cabin.[36] Old timers attribute it to a long ago trapper, but time has passed on and no, new, helpful information of who he or she was or when he or his family lived there has been made available, It is possible the cabin was used, at least for a few years, after the reservoir was finished as a set of crumbling steps can still be seen leading to the water's edge.

Oregon Trail Graves

Much has been written about the Oregon Trail and how important it was and is to the area around Guernsey and the State Park. In places the Oregon Trail ran through what is now within the boundaries of the park. The Trail stayed south and west of the river in this area. The Mormon Trail is located just north of the park, in places it is less than a mile from the parks border.

One of the most interesting developments of the Civilian Conservation Corps and the building of the park include accounts of graves in the park left behind from travellers on the Oregon Trail. It might be more speculation than history but a long time rumour or belief is that at one time there was reported research indicating there were graves within the park, upstream from what today is Sandy Beach, Sandy Point, and Sandy Cove campgrounds.[37] It is believed the graves were on the south side of North Platte River one or two miles upstream from the Narrows.

It is supposed, but not proven, this is why it is one of the wonderful mysteries of the park, that the CCC never developed the Sandy Beach area because of the graves. Years later the State Park System did develop the area as no clear evidence was offered of Oregon Trail burials in the area. If there were graves they are long forgotten and covered with water. For those who travelled the trail, a resting place in what has become Guernsey State Park would not be too bad.

The Historic Trail Ruts South of Guernsey

Camp BR-10, the Remains

The men of Company 1858 - Camp BR-10, and the architect for the Castle and Million Dollar Biffy, E.S. Moser, were moved away from Guernsey Lake State Park before they had finished everything that they planned and wanted to accomplish.[38] The only pieces remaining today of Camp BR-10 are the Powderhouse, several foundations and floors, outlines of roads and walkways, and what's left of a rather elaborate latrine.

It is fascinating to note that some modern park historians and a few of the newer publications on the park and park history note there are no remains of Camp BR-10, (publications and camp/park information from the 1980s and 1990s), yet it easy to find remains if an adventurer knows where to look. The area once occupied by the Camp has a small pull-off on the south side of Skyline Drive and a parking area for one or two cars. An interpretive sign can be found after reaching the site of the nicely preserved BR-10 Powderhouse.

The Powderhouse is well hidden, so well, in fact, that people driving past on Skyline drive will not notice it nestled among the rocks and trees of the north facing hill on the south side of the site of the old Camp.

Camp BR-10 Powderhouse

Walking through the area it is easy to imagine the way the old camp was setup. The camp was short lived, being barley finished when it was decommissioned and the men and buildings were moved to other camp sites. What is left today still tells a great story of what the camp looked like during its short existence. Enough is left to give a feel of CCC, Camp BR-10, and the less than two year time period they were in existence, living and working on the west side of the park.

Path in old Camp BR-10

Floors and Foundations from Old Camp BR-10

Chapter 4 –The Job at Guernsey

The general setup of the two camps within the boundaries of Guernsey State Park was left up to the Bureau of Reclamation. All work was to be for development of a park. The National Park Service was given the task of organizing and planning of the work in the park area. Work was to be completed by the two camps of 18 to 25 year old Civilian Conservation Corps laborers.[39]

Although the CCC men did the work, supervisors and craft experts were often hired from outside the CCC program. The two camps at Guernsey employed numerous laid-off workers from the nearby Sunrise Mine. *(The mine, now closed since the early 1980s, is located east of Hartville).* These men had great knowledge of explosives and moving rock. Local brick and stone masons from Guernsey, Hartville and Torrington were also utilized teaching men the particulars of laying stone and creating tight bonds between stones. Other locals taught bulldozer and motor grader skills to enrollees. These older men, hired by the government to train young enrollees, were referred to as LEMS, an acronym for Local Experienced Men Service. (Sometimes written as LEM)[40] This hiring of locals helped camps fit better into the communities near their working area. The number of LEMS, nationwide, would eventually grow to more than 30,000.

The men who made up the two Guernsey Lake camps were from the western part of the

United States. The men of BR-9 were moved, as a group, to Guernsey from Texas but were from many states including: Arizona, New Mexico, Oklahoma, and Colorado along with Wyoming. Once the two camps were established more local men became part of the CCC. Many of the new workers, in Civilian Conservation Corps camps nationwide were homesick, tired, and more than a bit confused by the time they arrived in camp, no matter where the camp was. The workers of BR-9 and BR-10 were no different.

Many of these young workers had roamed city streets or rural areas, looking for work, food, or handouts, sometimes out of desperation they looked for all three. A few rode the rails, portrayed in movies and books as carefree, relaxed and happy. But these men were not, in fact they traveled hungry, many walking or hitchhiking. Still others stayed at home trying to do what they could for their families. In a few instances early workers had hopes the CCC was a relief camp where they could sit around, do nothing, and get paid. Young men of the CCC soon found out this was a fallacy.

Photos and stories of CCC camps show military training and conditions but this wasn't always the practice. Conditions were strict when each new group of men arrived but as they adapted to camp life and the daily work and routine it became more like a civilian group on the job than a military one.

Men of Camp BR-10 Line up for Supper

Photo - Wyoming State Archives, Department of State Parks and Cultural Resources

After the first year the military thought it unwise, with trouble brewing in Europe, to have so many officers assigned duty with the Civilian Conservation Corps. President Roosevelt was in favor of the CCC being work camps and did not want them turned into pre-Army training centers. Of the two camps at Guernsey the newer, west side, Camp BR-10 was more of a strict military camp than was Camp BR-9 on the east side. After a year of activity the camps showed less resemblance to strict military establishments, much like camps around the nation.

This changed in 1941, several years after both Guernsey camps were gone, when most of the camps nationwide took on more of a military look and feel in preparation for the possible entry of the United States into World War Two.

Scores of camps, including Camp BR-10, were controlled by Army personnel. Camp BR-10 was headed by Captain F.W. Maxwell of the regular United States Army. This camp, because of Maxwell's army background, did have more of the look and feel of a military operation than did some camps around the nation.

Camp BR-10 Commander F. W. Maxwell

Photo - Wyoming State Archives, Department of State Parks and Cultural Resources

Camp BR-9, in contrast to Camp 10, was led by non-military, Project Superintendent James Coffman, who along with the rest of the camp, was paid from Civilian Conservation Corps or CB, not military, funds. Coffman did, at times, appear in military style CCC uniforms but was not active military during his tenure in Guernsey and most often dressed in the simple work clothes of the day.

J. H. COFFMAN
Project Superintendent

J. H. Coffman Camp BR-9 Leader

Photo - Wyoming State Archives, Department of State Parks and Cultural Resources

It is noteworthy that both camps fell under the general authority of the Bureau of Reclamation and worked on similar projects. Yet in some respects the two camps were quite different. The east side, Camp-9, was strictly CCC while the west side, Camp-10 was military/CCC. Although one camp was military and one not, the day to day operations were nearly identical. The only tangible difference was what part of the government the funding came from. When the newer of the camps, Camp 10, became a victim of budget cuts, and was closed, the workers of Camp 9 finished west side projects, including the Castle, that were in progress when the camp was moved out.[41]

The camps were, out of necessity, ran in a semi-military fashion which made for orderly use of camp facilities. When the men were working afield the atmosphere was one of relaxed hard work. While at work, the men were asked to think and practice, safety first. Early on the CCC experienced, nationwide, too many injuries and too many accidental deaths. By the time the camps were established in Guernsey, the safety first motto had become a daily part of life in the Civilian Conservation Corps. Superintendent Coffman noted the practice of safety first was working, recording only 12 lost time accidents out of 62,813 man-days in Camp BR-9. [42]

Many of the early CCC workers were less disciplined than were later hired workers. Working discipline was taught, or learned, by pride in workmanship and pride in accomplishments. Sometimes contests of, who can get the most done today, or this week, accomplished the goal. As projects were completed or starting to take shape, more and more, the men started to feel like they were accomplishing something of real value. [43]

When Camp BR-10 started, so did a healthy rivalry and competition between the two camps. This competition would prove to be quite challenging over the next two years. Elaborate bridges, the Million Dollar Biffy, *(the comfort station/restroom located near the Castle),* and other projects likely became bigger and bolder because of these contests. Trail making and speed to completion of trail miles may also have led to the intricate system of hiking trails in the park. Early stage planning also called for several miles of equestrian trails but if any of these were finished nothing was recorded in Coffman's notes, or on any of the Bureau of Reclamation maps.

Several of the early project maps showed dotted, unnamed lines that presumably were marked, but unbuilt trails.[44] If the dotted lines would have become trails they were mostly up on top, above Lakeshore Drive on the east side of the lake. The trail system today shows nine or ten miles of trails, but the wandering adventurer can still find several more miles of mostly unused and barley marked trail. With the addition of these trails the total mileage of trails in the park may be closer to the thirty plus miles the CCC had in mind for the trail system on the east side.[45]

Guernsey Fish Rearing Ponds

Possibly the shortest lasting of the projects completed by the Guernsey campers was started in the summer of 1935 and took place a few miles outside of the parks boundaries. The CCC was charged with building a fish rearing facility near the neighboring town of Guernsey. The area selected for the ponds was south of town about a half mile a mere one-hundred yards south of the North Platte River. The area was referred to as Island Park because a spring fed slough sided the area to the west and south. This area with the river close on the north and the slough circling on two sides seemed ideal.

Building the Ponds South of Guernsey

Photo - Wyoming State Archives, Department of State Parks and Cultural Resources

The men finished the building of nine fishponds complete with stone masonry gates. The sandy and rocky soil was dug out to a depth of four or five feet allowing some extra depth so the ponds could be lined with local clay to slow seepage. Although much hand work was involved the corps also used a gas shovel, several dump trucks, tractors and pickups building the ponds, gates, dams and roads within the Island Park fish rearing facility.

Despite the best efforts of the engineers and men of the camps the fish rearing ponds didn't last long. The idea had been to pump from the river, circulate through the ponds then into the slough that ran east for a half mile and dumped back into the North Platte River. The ponds failed, never able to hold enough water without constant pumping from the river.

Fishing Pond, once part of the CCCs Island Park
Is still a popular fishing hole

A few years after completion of the project the fish rearing ponds were left to memories. Today the area of the fish ponds can still be seen, standing as nine aging, sunken sentinels, saluting the work of the CCC and to the reality that all projects didn't make it. This area can be reached by taking the well-known road to the Oregon Trail Ruts Historical Site. This road is south of Guernsey over the river bridge with a right turn, to the west, about one hundred yards after crossing. The Trail Ruts turn off road is well marked.

The ponds are located a quarter of a mile east and north of the ruts. Today the ponds are bounded on the north by a well maintained gravel road leading to the Ruts and on the south by a fine, paved, walking trail. There is also a parking area for walkers, fisherman and history buffs bordering the ponds on the southeast.

A walking search of the area of Island Park will yield views of old gates, the depressions where ponds once held fish, and some interconnections between them.

For the most part, today, all of it is lost, even the name. Part of the slough south of the nine ponds is now a popular fishing area for kids or often grandparents and kids. But even this, now called by the generic name of the Guernsey Fish Pond, no longer reminds anyone of the CCC. Too bad. It is my hope that someday the area might be cleaned up and signage installed as a remembrance of something built by the CCC, something that almost worked. Today even the memories of Island Park Fish Facility are gone.

Guernsey Fish Rearing Station Head Gate

Working Camps the CCC Way

All of the projects and men of camps, BR-9 and BR-10, were first split into three general categories, engineering, agricultural and landscaping.[46] Each work group was headed by a foreman and assistant foreman. The group's foremen reported progress and problems to the camp superintendent. Engineering concentrated on the planning and architecture of structures, roads and trails in the park. The agricultural group cut and planted trees and reseeded areas finished by the landscaping crew. The landscaping crews moved rock and graded and raked for finishing touches and drainage. Groups often worked together, especially when it came to moving heavy rock and setting in place the massive peeled log timbers.

Projects for the engineers included undertakings as intricate as building the Museum, and as dangerous as the building and placing of guard rails along Lakeshore Drive. The agricultural groups planted more than five hundred trees, cleaned some five acres of beach and cut brush along with general clean-up throughout the park.[47]

The landscapers were responsible for building or finishing work on numerous parking areas, fences and trails. They also were the lead on shaping drainage away from camping and picnicking areas. Working together the agriculture and landscaping crews placed interpretive and informational signs around the park. Park signs ranged from simple wood painted black with silver lettering to more worker intensive log engraved signs that could weigh more than 100 pounds.

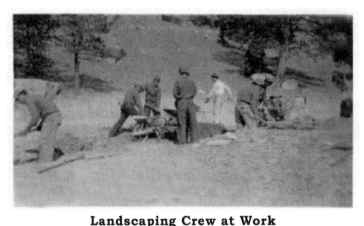

Landscaping Crew at Work
Photo – Wyoming State Archives, Department of State Parks and Cultural Resources

The crews also built numerous cut stone fire places in the park. These were beautifully made and would have taken much time and many hours of labor. Today some can still be found, but all of these firepits are out of service.

Remains of a CCC built Cut Stone Fire Pit

Notes on work completed by Camp BR-9 list their many accomplishments: buildings, latrines, shelters, guard rails, power lines, water and sewer lines, drinking fountains, fireplaces, signs, tables, roads, trails, parking areas, pull off areas, rock quarrying, surveying and map work, docks and a floating swimming pier, culverts and stone drainage ditches, bridges, grass and tree planting, fire pits and general clean up.[48] This is not a complete list but should give readers the feel for much of what was going on with the CCC camps at Lake Guernsey.

Road Builders on a hot summer day
Photo – Wyoming State Archives, Department of State Parks and Cultural Resources

Working in swimming suits demonstrates strict military regulations were not always part of the CCC work crew's daily routine.

Chapter 5 – The Workers

A Day in the Life of a CCC Worker

By 1935 there were 2,650 CCC camps in the United States with camps located in all of the forty-eight states. Young men, most with their first real job earned thirty dollars a month. Although a good number of people called this salary a dollar a day, it is not strictly true as weekends were off for the CCC men. This would mean most worked twenty to twenty five days per month, making their pay slightly more than a dollar a day. On a national level there were some protests, thinking this salary too low, even for what many believed was a government handout. For the most part the men were happy to have work and no records, which I have run across, report organized protests from workers in any of the Civilian Conservation Corps camps.

Of the $30.00 the men were paid, they were allowed to keep $5.00, the rest was sent home as relief for CCC member families. The $25.00 each workers family received every month was one of the first real attempts in America to jump start the economy during the hard times of the Great Depression.

The five dollars the workers kept each month might not sound like much in present day, but in the 1930s the men were able to buy camp vouchers used to purchase articles at the camp store. Any money left was used during weekend trips to town.

Building Lakeshore Drive
Photo – Wyoming State Archives, Department of State Parks and Cultural Resources

In fact the men of the camps at Guernsey Lake spent some of their weekend time, in the town of Guernsey, enjoying life away from the camp, and experiencing a few other places to spend their precious little cash.

Generally workers from Civilian Conservation Corps camps were accepted in the towns and cities nearby. Guernsey like all CCC camp towns did have trouble, at times, when the workers went to town.[49] Several east side trail maps show an unnamed and unidentified trail breaking off from Red Cliff Trail and leading toward the town of Guernsey.[50] It is believed the trail ran to southeast to the Kelley's Park area then followed the river into Guernsey.

**View from Round Top Mountain of the CCC Mystery
Trail into Guernsey**

A trail such as this could have been built and used by workers bored with CCC night life who wanted to get into town for a taste of Guernsey after hours. There are undocumented stories of fights and a knifing taking place between CCC workers and young men from town.[51] One story relates the tale of a rope or rope ladder being used to climb cliffs to escape townspeople following workers back to camp, presumably to get, "a piece of their hide." The mysterious trail ends on the east side of Camp BR-9, Company 844.[52]

The Routine

For the working men every day started as a repeat of the day before. Each day began with the sounding of reveille at 6:00 AM sharp. Unlike the fine sounding trumpet of movies, reveille ranged from a record played through scratchy speakers to trumpets played with varying amounts of talent from camp musicians. On occasion, when a camp found itself without a way to sound the familiar wake up, a camp counselor substituted a walk through the camp blowing a whistle to wake up the men. Even when musicians were available the tune might be the unmistakable, reveille call, but played much slower than the accustomed beat, playing up to tempo was difficult for lesser accomplished musicians, but any form of the song was acceptable in camp. Most didn't want to get up no matter how the song sounded, but they all got up, after-all it was breakfast time.

After, reveille, a camp counselor walked through the barracks to make sure everyone was getting out of bed. At 6:30 AM the men stood at attention for the raising of the American flag and roll call. They then returned to barracks to make their beds and wash-up. Men were required to be clean and presentable at all times, including clean and combed hair, brushed teeth and a shower at a minimum of once each week.

Many authoritative sources mention the average CCC man was nearly 20 years old and came from a large family where his father was unemployed. Average education was only at the eighth grade level, although in that day this was not as unusual as it might be today. This, mister average CCC man, was around five feet eight inches tall and weighed slightly less than 150 pounds.[53]

Most workers came from reasonably stable blue collar homes where their father had worked for hourly or weekly wages but was now unemployed.

Camp clothing was furnished by the government and was the same in every camp. Blue denim for work and army olive drab uniforms for dress were furnished by the CCC and the only clothes to be worn in camp. Before any readers start to believe the men were perfectly groomed and dressed each day, consider their green work uniforms, leftover surplus from WWI, by then twenty years in the past.

In 1938, Roosevelt felt like the olive drab Civilian Conservation Corps uniform was too army like. He ordered new spruce green dress uniforms. With the CCC nicknamed the Tree Army, they now looked even more like the nickname fit the organization.

Breakfast was at 7:00 sharp, and like most things in camp it was an organized affair. The men marched in pairs to the mess hall and lined up for their morning meal. Meals in the camp were made up of a considerable amount of wholesome and filling food. A typical breakfast might include fruit, eggs, bacon or ham, cereal, fresh bread and coffee.

The men of the CCC never went hungry.

Mess Hall - Camp BR-10

Photo – Wyoming State Archives, Department of State Parks and Cultural Resources

By 7:45 breakfast was completed and camp officers were busy inspecting bunks, quarters and foot lockers. If everything was neat and orderly, as expected, the men were sent off to work at 8:00 AM. If anything was not as it should be men were required to cleanup or, make appropriate, whatever was found as in error by the inspectors. If problems were found it was noted and the campers were reminded to not let it happen again. Camps used a demerit system and men could be released from their job with the CCC if they received too many demerits.

The two camps at Guernsey, like most camps, were divided into three types of work groups. Select groups centered on road and trail building and stone work. Others like the landscapers worked on projects throughout the soon to be State Park. They walked or were taken by truck to the site of their work for the day. Workers at Guernsey were normally feed a hot lunch, or in that day what they called dinner at the local camps, then trucked back to work.

When the job, such as building the fish rearing ponds at Island Park south of Guernsey, took the crews too far to conveniently bring them back for dinner, sack lunches were provided. The sack lunches varied little. The usual sack contained two sandwiches and a piece of fruit or some type of raw vegetable. Coffee and water were provided to wash it down. Working men, regardless if they were in camp or out on the job were given one full hour for lunch. Far away from the camp there was still time enough to make a pot of coffee at lunch and the workers took advantage of this with the CCC providing the coffee, coffee pot and generally a cook to make it. They may have been the first Americans to have coffee delivered to the jobsite.

The work day ended at 4:00 and the men were expected to clean-up and change from their work clothes into camp clothing. This gave the men plenty of free time before the evening meal, supper, a little after six. Men rested, talked, played catch and generally got to know one another during this time.

Each evening at 6:00 PM the men, once again, lined up at the flag pole, this time for the lowering of the stars and stripes and the playing of, *Retreat*. After the folding of the flag the men were marched to the mess hall for their evening meal. Unlike cafeteria lines common to the military, the workers of the CCC sat in their assigned seats and were served by men given that duty for the week. KP was rotated among the workers with kitchen duties ranging from peeling potatoes to helping the cooks and serving in the mess hall.

Supper, after a good days work, was always large, roast beef, pork or chicken, potatoes and gravy, vegetables and fruit. Meals included, bread and butter and most often a selection of jellies and jams. Camp leaders and cooks tried to vary the diet of the men but most food was still considered the common filling fare of the day. Many of the men in CCC camps were undernourished or close to it when they joined but gained weight during their employment. A few camps reported they had enlistees who were able to add ten to twenty pounds during one six month enlistment period.[54]

The list of foods sent out to the camps was quite long, camps bought locally when possible. They not only bought from local groceries but also purchased from local meat markets and at times direct from local producers. Food item purchase lists included: beef, pork, chicken, turkey, fish, flour, lard, butter, milk, onions, squash, potatoes, rice, sugar, syrup, apples, baking powder, yeast, cinnamon, cocoa, corn, beans, macaroni, peaches, peas, pepper, pickles, pineapple, prunes, both dry and stewed, rolled oats, salt, tea, pepper, ginger, coffee, tomatoes, and vinegar.[55] In camps where it was possible the men frequently grew large productive gardens.

The Post Exchange

After supper the Post Exchange, the men called it the Canteen, opened with usual hours from 7:30 to 9:00 PM, some camps stretched this for the men, opening at seven or a quarter after and sometimes stretching it out until 9:30. The Post Exchange offered candy, soda pop, tooth paste, tobacco products, hair oil and many other needed or desired items.

The Exchange ran on a system of vouchers the men called tickets, they were able to purchase a single, two dollar packet of vouchers at a time. No money was exchanged for these tickets. The price was simply deducted from their months' pay. Still, the limit was five dollars as this was all the, keep in pocket, money campers were allowed each month. It was suggested and common for the men to buy two packets of tickets, one at the first of the month and one in the middle of the month, and save a dollar for town money. Money made from sales in the canteen stayed in the camp and was used to purchase athletic equipment and uniforms. The money was also used as funding for startups, or to keep in production, camp newspapers. The newspaper for Guernsey CCC was appropriately named the, *"The Dam Site News."*

Most workers were satisfied with the five dollars a month they had to spend at the Post Exchange. Not only did five dollars go much farther in the 1930s than it does today, the men received other benefits. Each man in addition to the $30.00 per month pay received clothing, board and room, free doctoring and haircuts for a few cents. And the doctor and barber came to them, setting up shop in the Exchange.

In the two Guernsey camps Friday night was entertainment night at the recreation hall. The two camps joined together for these performances and the public was not only invited to attend but encouraged to participate. Each Friday evening's entertainment started promptly at 7:30.

According to one local newspaper the, *Torrington Telegram,* performances included everything from educational talks, to singing, dancing, boxing and wrestling.[56] Each evening's program was separated into three categories, athletic, educational and recreational. After a hard week of working in the park, entertainment night was a much looked forward to event.

Library Study Room
Photo - Wyoming State Archives, Department of State Parks and Cultural Resources

Only a few, if any, bad reports came from the men of the CCC. The work was hard but gratifying and the pay helped not only the worker but his family as well. Life was good for the men of the Corps. Their time went fast and was limited to four hitches of six months each. Not many workers served four hitches spending two full years in the corps. But early on more than half of the men re-upped at least once. Each camp at Guernsey featured wooden barracks and a well done recreation hall, complete with a canteen.

Numerous camps, including the two at Guernsey, also offered educational buildings including, libraries, classrooms and learning centers.

The recreation hall at Camp BR-9 had two pool tables, a ping pong table, a library, with a reading room and a massive red sandstone fireplace. BR-10 wasn't in existence long enough to be elaborate but their recreation hall and canteen had pool and ping pong tables and a library with reading and study areas.

Libraries were well stocked for their time and locations, but were criticized by some. Library critics felt the reading material was too centered on adventure, mystery and westerns, and not enough of the classics. As a long time teacher and researcher I am not sure the classics would have seen as much use in these camps as genre fiction. The men did spend a considerable amount of reading time looking at popular magazines of the day, as evidenced by the long lists of magazine subscriptions delivered to the camp.

Library-Study Area

Photo – Wyoming State Archives, Department of State Parks and Cultural Resources

Men who had energy left at the end of the day often participated in sports. Pick-up baseball games were a part of each camp. Hiking, recreational climbing and exploration of nearby park areas were popular among the men. The tennis court, areas to toss horse-shoes and open areas to play catch were all made available to the men. The local camps had basketball hoops on dirt courts and the canteen offered cards and table games during its open hours.

Camp BR-10 Softball Team
Photo - Wyoming State Archives, Department of State Parks and Cultural Resources

Many camps sponsored traveling basketball, baseball or softball teams but most camp sports were recreational and intramural only, played for fun not skill. Camp BR-9 had a traveling baseball team for at least two summers. Camp BR-10 was short lived but did sport a softball team. In some camps, none in Wyoming, workers were recruited because of their skill playing sports instead of their worker talents.

Lights-out in CCC camps was at 10 o'clock. The men were given a warning 15 minutes earlier. In most camps bed checks were made at 11 o'clock nightly. Late in the years of the CCC, with desertion becoming a more common occurrence, guards were often out and about from ten until early morning. The guards were a determent but were not armed and did not have much authority other than to tell men to go back to bed. These were not military camps, they did not want newly trained men to leave, but it sometimes happened. The CCC, throughout its active years, had waiting lists but that meant continually training new, green, recruits.

New Men Lining up at Camp BR-9
Photo - Wyoming State Archives, Department of State Parks and Cultural Resources

Chapter 6 – Fun in the Park

The Water Carnivals

The water carnival, sponsored by the Lake Guernsey Boat Club, was an event held for several years on the lake. The carnival was not a CCC affair but the Corps played a large part in making these memorable events possible. The first of several, Lake Guernsey Water Carnivals, was held, August 11, 1935.

The First Water Carnival

Photo - Wyoming State Archives, Department of State Parks and Cultural Resources

The newly built Lakeshore Drive allowed people to get into the recreational areas of the lake for the first time. And wow, did they come. Reports indicate over 20,000 spectators showed up for that first day's activities.[57] CCC men directed traffic, handed out information and directed cars to parking areas.

RACING BOATS AT THE WATER CARNIVAL SPONSORED BY THE LAKE GUERNSEY BOAT CLUB. AUGUST 11, 1935

Photo - Wyoming State Archives, Department of State Parks and Cultural Resources

Individual workers, who could, did their work, then sat back and enjoyed a terrific summer show. It took so many workers to put on the carnivals that when the CCC ended in Guernsey, so did the huge water show.

Events for the water carnival included such things as, speed boat races, rowing competitions, swimming races and a bathing beauty contest.

WATER SPORTS AT THE LAKE GUERNSEY BOAT CLUB
WATER CANIVAL.

Photo - Wyoming State Archives, Department of State Parks and Cultural Resources

Expanding the Park

The carnivals were so well attended that considerable discussion was held on expanding the brand new area of the park. It was believed Lake Guernsey Park was so special it could become the most popular tourist area on the east side of the state. Expansion talk centered on the land to the north of the park, an area that would take in more historical and geological sites. If the expansion would have been carried out the Spanish Diggings, Immigrant Hill, the mysterious chimneys to the northwest, Crystal Cave and Sawmill Canyon would have been part of the park. Planners believed with proper development this may have made for quite a remarkable visiting and vacationing area.

Possibly Guernsey State Park would have been a serious rival for vacationing and tourism to the present day Black Hills of South Dakota. Today, Sawmill Canyon, Crystal Cave, the ancient chimneys and most of the Immigrant Hill area are on dangerous artillery range, military land, and out of bounds for tourists.

Brimmer Point and the Carnival

Brimmer Point, reached by turning from the CCC constructed Skyline Drive, and easy to see from Lakeshore Drive, was used a few years for a crowd pleasing carnival event. Each year the crowd eagerly awaited the amazing push the car off the point and into the lake event. It's difficult to believe today that they did this, but for the first few years of the carnival this event was one of the highlights for the day. This may have been the early day predecessor to the crash up or wreck up derbies popular at fairs and events around the country in present time.

Brimmer Point to the Lake – a long drop

Picturing the car tumbling off the cliff, maybe it would have been fun to watch. I'm not sure park personnel, who were charged with clean up, were sad to see this event fade to a memory. After a year or two of pushing the car off the cliff it ended. When one crazy event ended another, often just as crazy, started.

One year a rope was stretched from Brimmer Point across the lake and anchored on the east side boat dock area. A daredevil would then slide down the rope, like an old fashioned version of zip lining, but he would release from the rope in the middle of the lake and drop 100 feet into the water. This event was only allowed once, and instead of a death defying act it was a spoof. Several boats waited in the water for the man dropping but instead it was a dummy that dropped. The dummy was pushed off Brimmer Point down the quickly descending rope attached to a small wire release. When the fake daredevil reached a certain point the release was triggered. As the dummy tumbled toward the lake a man in one of the boats rolled out into the water, the weighted down dummy sank and the new man in the water, popped up, and appeared to be the intrepid risk-taker who released from the zip line. Viewers were astounded by the feat, but it ended, thankfully, after one year.

Records do not tell how long after the daredevil stunt the viewer's found out they were hoodwinked. In that time and place I am sure spectators enjoyed a good laugh and maybe a sigh of relief when they found out it was nothing more than a simple trick.

A few parts of the carnivals survived, although somewhat smaller after the CCC left the park. When World War II came the carnivals went away, forever. Various summer water events are still staged throughout the park but the last attempts for any type of water carnival happened with a short lived revival in the late 1980s. The new version of the carnival featured, sand volleyball, free boat tours of the lake and the ability to try out individual water craft and boats from area vendors. The event was well attended, although nowhere near the reported 20,000 from the first water carnival, but with worries of insurance and lawsuit problems for vendors it ended after a run of two years.

Today triathlete type events, along with rock climbing, road racing and mountain biking are popular competitive and recreational park activities.

A Young Climber Tests His Rock Climbing at Lower Levels

Chapter 7 - Stories of the Park

Short Stories of the Park

Civilian Conservation Corps workers were encouraged to read and to spend time writing while in the corps. Writing paper and pencils were furnished free of charge and diaries were available for purchase at the canteen with camp vouchers. Some men who had taken little interest in school spent time writing letters home and later some kept journals of their day to day activities. Classes were available to members who wanted to become better readers or writers.

A few men began to write poetry and short stories and some became self-styled novelists. Not every camper became an accomplished writer, but with the time, help from camp staff, and maturity, some men became writers who left behind a legacy of stories from the CCC.

Around the nation CCC camps were putting out newspapers, many generically titled, *"Happy Days."* The newspaper at Guernsey was fortunate when workers came up with their own name for a paper and the, *"Dam Site News,"* was born. Camp newspapers were published and read throughout the Civilian Conservation Corps with some stories getting picked up and reprinted in popular newspapers across America and abroad.

The following two stories are an acknowledgement to camp newspapers throughout the Civilian Conservation Corps. *"This Job Ain't Half*

Bad," and, *"Hey, Let's Build a Castle,"* are works of fiction but based on tales from the two CCC camps that built Guernsey State Park. Although fictionalized, the short stories are based on several variations of the same camp life events. Parts of the stories survived, barely, as oral history. It is my wish that an oral history type retelling here will help them live on.

The following stories are my works of fiction, all characters and names are products of the author's imagination, places and events are based on oral history and local folklore. Any resemblance to real persons, living or dead, is purely coincidental.

Thank you and enjoy this fictional part of the CCC story.

Neil Waring

This Job Ain't Half Bad - August 1936

"This job is worse than starving to death."

I looked over at Howard, but didn't say anything, just nodded and I might have smiled a little. Work was hard for Company 844 at Camp BR-9, and the weather was crazy, not like Texas. Not like Texas at all. We wake up freezing, melt in the middle of the day heat, and then freeze at night.

I was never sure if Howard, we all called him Howie, he didn't like us calling him that at first but then he sort of got used to it, anyway as I was saying, I wasn't ever sure when Howard was telling the truth or when he was stretching it out some. He was always telling us he wished he was back riding the rails when he just kept moving on.

As for him saying the job was worse than starvin', well, I'll just say I never seen him back off none from food in the chow hall. Seemed any of his five dollars he had left after buying tobacco and fixin's he spent on candy and soda pop down at the canteen. No, he liked to eat and he ate a lot.

Lights were to be out at nine in the camp and when nine came the lights went out. On one such night, at three quarters past nine, Howie was gone. These places were not Army Camps, but you weren't supposed to sneak out at night, especially with Captain Cruse looking out. When reveille sounded at 6:30 A.M. there he was rubbing his eyes and stretching and scratching like the rest of us.

We marched two by two down the path to the flag rasin' and on into the mess hall for breakfast. They sure didn't spare any on feedin' us, that's for sure. We ate eggs, sausage, fresh bread and jelly and lots of hot coffee with plenty of sugar to touch it up, us Texas boys really appreciated the sweet coffee on cold mornings.

It wasn't till we got in the truck for the ride down the road that I got a chance to talk to Howie. But he shushed me with a, "shhheeee," and whispered, "later."

Well, by now I was really wondering where ol' Howie spent some of the night, the part where I didn't see him. Knowing Howie like I do, him being my best friend and all, it was sure going to be some tale.

I don't mean to say Howie was some kind of liar or something but his stories did seem to get bigger and better with every telling. Now, I don't know a lot about life, beings as I just lived in Texas and now Wyoming. But the way I figure it, if his stories get better each time, well maybe, the first tellin' shied away from the truth a mite and the second tellin' was better because he told the entire true story. But I don't think so.

The two of us had been working with landscaping since we arrived at BR-9, to the government landscaping meant moving rocks, lots of rocks. Ol' Howie, he's quite the joker, said he wrote home and told his folks he'd made four good friends the first week he was in camp. Said Phil, that's me, and three guys he thought might be brothers, pick, shovel and rake, said he told them he thought their last name was Blisters.

Howie always made for good stories but I don't really think he would have written that, least ways not to his mom and pop. I know I sure wouldn't, and especially wouldn't write that stuff here in this personal and true diary of my experiences in the CCC. Don't get me wrong, this isn't going to be a book or anything like that. I just wanted to write down what was happening every day here at the camp. Some day in seventy or eighty years these stories might be fun to read. I sure hope so.

We'd been on this road building, landscaping, and rock moving crew, for three months and three days. I know because of my journal-un. My old teachers sure would be surprised to see how good I have become when I set down with paper and pencil.

Finally we stopped and got out of the truck and grabbed our tools, Howie's best friends, the blister boys, and started to rake and move rock.

That's when I was finally able to talk in private with Howie. "Howie where'd you go off to last night after lights out?" I asked.

"What you mean, I was right there in my bunk cross from you, just like every other night."

Then I gave him my look, least way Ma said I had a look, not a mad look, more of a look like, I ain't believin' what I'm hearing look.

Howie smiled, looked around and said, "had to slip out, needed a smoke and to use the latrine, that's all."

So I gives him the look again, and he squinted through the bright sunlight at me and says, "No."

I said, "Nope, you weren't there an hour later either."

He lets out a big breath of air, starts rolling a smoke and says, "Did anyone else see me, I had some business in town?"

At last we were getting somewhere. We went to town every weekend, usually on Saturday's early in the forenoon so we could get back for movie night, pretty good movies too, and only a dime to get a seat. I tossed a scoopful of rocks over the bank and watched them tumble into the lake. Sometimes I wondered if by the time we got the road finished the lake might be full of rock. "What kind of business you have in town, we get in every week or so, never seen you doing any business other than ogling the town girls like the rest of us."

"Game, crap game, they have one every Tuesday night, usually goes on most of the night, up by the tracks, west of the roundhouse. I knew the dice would be hot, hot enough that I would be shed of this place by morning, almost did too."

"What happened," I said, "dice cool off?"

Before he could answer, I knew what answer was coming but his tellin' of it might be fun.

"Never was hot, lost the only dollar I had and the dollar I borrowed off of you, only took three-quarters of an hour and I was walking back, got back so fast I still got a pretty good night's sleep."

I couldn't help myself, just started laughing, the rest of the crew turned and looked at us but figured it was just Howie and one of his stories making' me laugh. I looked over at him and told him, "Ya know Howie, you remind me of that old sayin'." Then I left it alone, kind of baiting him.

He took the bait, "what sayin' is that, he said."

"You know, if it weren't for bad luck I wouldn't have any luck at all." Even ol' Howie had to smile at that one.

Hope this gives you an idea of some of the goings on and what it was like at camp BR-9.

We had plenty of hot food, lots of hard work and a good helping of shenanigans.

This ends my little story of CCC camp life.

Philip P. Palmer.

Oh, and one more thing, they moved us off the road the next morning and we went up behind the Museum and started building a golf course. Howie says he thinks he could learn how to play golf, then maybe bet money against guys, thinks he could win enough to get out of here, that Howie, he's always thinking.

Post Script – I signed up for another six month hitch when my time was up, and darned if they didn't send me to write camp stories for the newspaper, *"The Dam Site News."* I never saw Howie again, said he was heading to Nevada, thought that it might be the next big boom area. He believed it might be a place to make some, "real money."

I think he may have missed on this one. I haven't been there, but have heard Nevada is all desert with no people.

~END~

The Trail to Town

"Hey, Let's Build a Castle" - November 1936

If this were an old fashioned western novel the first words would be something like this. It all started when. . . . But it's not, nevertheless, please read on.

It all started on July 6, 1934, when two new recruits, Jimmy Robertson and Bill Heart got off the truck at Lake Guernsey, Camp BR-9. Fifteen minutes later they had their orders, and the first order - a two mile, or so, walk. The walk turned into a hike that would wind a Billy-goat, Jimmy and Bill remembered complaining all the way and perhaps they had reason to complain. The walk took them a half mile downhill, across the dam, up another half mile long hill, and that was the easy part. What was left, more than a mile up the side of a small mountain and down the other? With the hike complete they were in the place they would spend the next half year, or more if they wanted it, of their young lives – Camp BR-10, on the west side of Guernsey Lake.

Jimmy and Bill or Billy as everyone would soon call him, thought they had reason to complain, the hike was grueling, they didn't remember signing up for anything grueling.

One week later the two eighteen year olds rested in the dappled pine tree shade of an early mountain evening. Billy smiled, started to say something, muffled a laugh then said, "Well, we signed up for the job and our first job was to get to the job site or something like that."

Funny how conversations happen, the boys hadn't talked of the long hike since the day they made it, now out of the blue Billy brought it up again. Everything changed the morning after they arrived complaining of the hike. After a full five day week of working for the CCC they realized that every day was going to be hard, and now as they looked back that hike wasn't too bad.

Both young men, like so many of the unskilled new workers, were assigned to the road, trail and bridge crew, the work was hard, hot, dirty and in a few weeks both men would believe, rewarding, and maybe a little fun. Life had changed in the first weeks of their six month enlistment, changed exactly the way the CCC program wished and expected, for the better.

Three months later and half way through their enlistments the boys were tan, healthy and well fed for the first time in longer than either cared to admit.

Jimmy was moved over to construction part way through his second month and later Billy was moved from roads to the stone laying and building part of the construction crew. This meant both would be working on the shelter on the North Bluff, the one everyone was talking about. The boys over on the east side had been building three impressive structures for over a year, the new shelter they were building, called Sitting Bull, was a highly crafted stone and log structure that seemed to grow right out of the ground. The work took skill, time and a great deal of planning.

The men of BR-10 had been talking for weeks, saying their shelter on the North Bluff would be bigger and better than anything on the east side. The east side also was working on a huge limestone building that would become the park Museum. The workers on the west side didn't want to be outdone. After considerable talk and twisting of arms, a new plan was allowed for the North Bluff Shelter and because the east side had two buildings, the west side would also.

Unfortunately two buildings looked impossible, they had plans for only one. And then Jimmy realized something, something even the bosses were missing, they did have two buildings, a shelter and a comfort station. Comfort station being the governments highfalutin, words for outhouse. When Jimmy brought it up, everyone agreed, and the men cheered when one of the construction crew foreman said, "You're right, by golly, we will build the fanciest outhouse, sorry, comfort station the governments ever seen."

Billy could hardly contain himself blurting out, "yea, let's build a stone outhouse, a million dollar outhouse, and we can call it the great stone biffy on the bluff, should fit pretty well with huge picnic shelter.

One of the older men, he must have been near 24 or 25, slouched in the corner, said just loud enough for us to hear, "you mean a Million Dollar Biffy." And so it was, the Million Dollar Biffy on the North Bluff.

In their second enlistment Jimmy moved up to foreman, his crew in charge of moving rock from the quarry three quarters of a mile to the south of the bluff. Billy was the head-man of stone setting on the shelter and Biffy. It was interesting to watch the work proceed; building the Biffy and the Shelter at the same time. Work continued right along on the North Bluff but it was slow.

Early April brought more intense sunshine and a wind that howled out of the northwest, a nice fire burned in the great fireplace of the shelter for all the working hours and had been burning, every day, since its completion in December. By this time Jimmy and Billy believed their days in the CCC might end soon, the end of their enlistments in July was not far away, they had much to think about, much to discuss.

By the first of June they had made their decisions, both would leave the corps in July after a year as part of what they now thought was the greatest program the government had ever came up with. As their enlisted days drew to an end, and feeling a bit of melancholy, the two, now friends for life, asked the foreman if they could camp on the North Bluff for a couple of nights instead of going back to camp quarters.

The request was too much for the foreman, or as he put it, "The answer to your question is way above my pay grade."

Their request went to Captain Maxwell the Camp -10 superintendent. After listening to their reasoning, and shaking his head several times in the process he reluctantly agreed to let them camp. He told those who asked, "These lads worked here long enough to become men and then leaders of men. They're two of our most senior workers and have been at work since the beginning of the building on the North Bluff. This will give them a chance to say a fitting goodbye to their hard work, and I wish them well."

The first night was cool when they made up their bedrolls on the rock floor of the shelter in front of a roaring fire. The second night was pleasant, even warm, and the good friends chose to sleep on the flat prairie a few yards south and east of the shelter. Here out on the flat was a fire pit where many CCC boys had heated Coffee or sandwiches on days they had no ride back to camp for the noon diner. Today they built a huge fire, much more than they needed, then let it die back some not wanting the men of the camp, two miles below, to think they had started the mountain on fire.

The two young men talked far into the night and Jimmy, a developing self-proclaimed poet, read some of his verse, none of which Billy understood, but did allow that it sounded pretty.

Interesting how men can change with work and good food. Jimmy could barely read a year ago when he joined the CCC, the camp brought in help for those who wanted it. He wanted to read and write better and now here he was, some kind of CCC poet. Every evening in camp Jimmy read and read and read and then he started writing, now he reads and writes and reads and writes more than anyone in camp, likely more than anyone in America.

Camping on the North Bluff, it didn't take him long and sure enough Jimmy had penciled out the rough draft of a poem.

> *Against the backdrop of white cliffs and pine wood*
> *Sets a stone and log structure that if only it could*
> *It would be a castle, the great North Bluff Castle*
> *Awaiting ladies distressed and knights on bended knee*
> *Built by shinning green armored lads of the CCC*

The next day Billy couldn't get Jimmies verse out of his mind, kept calling the North Bluff Shelter the Castle. After that day everyone was laughing and saying they were building a Castle. They were never sure if the name stuck or not, they left a few weeks later, but for the rest of their lives they certainly enjoyed telling anyone who asked, "What did you do when you were in the CCC?"

"We built a Castle."

~END~

Chapter 8 – Parkitecture

The Rustic Architecture Movement in the Park

Guernsey State Park becoming one of the centerpieces of Rustic Architecture in the west is a direct result of the National Park Service (NPS) working with the Bureau of Reclamation to create usable recreation facilities around the Bureau's new Guernsey reservoir.[58] The CCC gave the National Park Service the perfect blank canvas to develop their skills for additional building in the nation's parks.

The NPS, founded in 1916, sought to build park facilities in a rustic manner without interrupting the surroundings. To build in this way, in concordance with natural surroundings and beauty, required a great amount of hand labor. Above all else it required taking away the usual symmetry of modern building. Native rock and timber became a cornerstone of this style.

Landscape architect Thomas C. Vent with the aid of Herbert Mairer were leaders in getting the idea of Rustic Architecture and rustic landscape design into the National Park Service.[59] Rustic Architecture featured massive peeled log and stone construction. This type of building was both time and hand labor intensive. With the end of the frontier in the west it was thought this style exemplified the pioneer spirit of the old west. The distinctive rustic buildings provide parks long lasting, beautiful and functional facilities.[60]

Log and Timber at Sitting Bull Shelter

Log construction with stone foundations and strong uneven rock or log walls with over-hanging roofs and small windows set-off the Rustic Movement from other types of architecture. Rustic building featured stone chimneys instead of the newer use of metal stove pipe. The movement did take advantage of the use of more manufactured materials for door and window frames. Some of these frames were prebuilt in a factory setting which speeded construction of the buildings. Rustic building also used more of the craftsman style, hip roof, something rarely used in log construction.

Massive Stone Fireplace in the Museum

&

Curved Lines of the Castle entry

Buildings of the rustic style are easily identifiable. Rustic buildings have lines, as all buildings must, but rustic lines harmonize with nature and appear to be so natural that they arise from the ground. Rustic Architecture attempted to stay away from the straight lines and the unnatural appearance of city housing.

Today both the Arts and Crafts Style and the Picturesque Style of the late 1700s and early 1800s can be found in parts of the Rustic Movement. The Picturesque Style involves the landscape around the structure more than many types of architecture and this would likewise become a distinction of the rustic style.

The rustic idea of landscape design was used, not only in the buildings of Guernsey State Park, but throughout the park in the design of park roads and its extensive trail system. This style helped hide roads and trails behind hills, trees and shrubs using natural local materials. Things that blended with, instead of standing out from the surrounding area. In more modern times this style is sometimes referred to as Naturalistic or Naturalistic design.

Knight Mountain Trail - Rustic and Natural

Two trails on the west side of the park feature rustic walking bridge design, the Brimmer Point Trail and Tunnel Mountain Trail. Both bridges feature beautifully completed rock and peeled log construction. Unfortunately both bridges were destroyed by the 2012 fire, a fire started by a thoughtless and preventable act. The bridges, at least the wooden parts, were destroyed by fire before and rebuilt. Everyone who hikes or mountain bikes in the park now eagerly anticipates the time when these bridges will once again be rebuilt to be enjoyed for many years to come.

Brimmer Point Trail Bridge after the Fire

Two wonderful road bridges on Lakeshore Drive are prominently rustic design. These bridges, the only two vehicle bridges on the east side of the park, are preserved and appear today much like the day they were designed and built. The foremost change was preparing the decking for a paved asphalt topping instead of the gravel used in construction of the original road and used for decades.

CCC Bridge on Lakeshore Drive

Rustic Design Summery

The State Park Museum and the Castle are the best examples of the rustic park building style in the park. Many more park projects including the four powder-houses, the Million Dollar Biffy, Sitting Bull Picnic Shelter and the viewing area at Brimmer Point are also terrific examples of Rustic Architecture. Trails were built, trees and shrubs were planted or removed with the rustic look of the park in mind. Smaller examples abound in the park with drinking fountains, fireplaces, shelters, culverts, rock walls and rock drainage areas, all truly rustic design.

Rustic Walls and Steps at Brimmer Point

Chapter 9 – The CCC

Civilian Conservation Corp – A Short History

Shortly after being sworn in as the nation's 32nd President, Franklin Roosevelt called Congress into Emergency Session and began the process of enacting his programs to put Americans back to work. His goal? To put an end to the Great Depression. The Civilian Conservation Corps, and multiple other relief programs were part of his ground breaking, New Deal. Senate Bill S-598 was introduced on March 27, 1933 and signed by the president four days later. Thirty-seven days after Roosevelt took the oath of office the first young man was signed up for the CCC.

Through the combined efforts of the United States Army, the Departments of Agriculture, Interior and Labor the Civilian Conservation Corps became a reality. The CCC was like nothing else ever created by the federal government. It had no book of rules, only the law that created it. The CCC would eventually enroll over 3,000,000 men, the leaders simply making it up as they went along, and it worked. The CCC ran as smooth as any government agency then or now.[61]

Robert Fechner was named the first director of the CCC. Fechner worked under the direct supervision of the four cabinet departments that organized and supervised the CCC. The Department of Labor recruited the men, the Army, under the War Department organized and ran the day to day activities of the camps. Two departments, Interior and Agriculture supervised Civilian Conservation Corps projects.[62] The only glitch in the system would be with FDR, the founder himself.

As Roosevelt's years in office progressed he often didn't have time to look over the paper work for each camp site, of which he had final approval. He got to them as soon as he could but the signups outpaced the opening of new camps. At times Roosevelt allowed Fechner to make the decisions on camp locations, but not often, especially early in the life of the camps. This was FDRs pet project and he made as many of the location decisions as he had time for.

Seems like FDR knew what would make a great site for a park. Indeed Guernsey's Park development with the CCC was authorized early in his presidency so it is likely President Roosevelt himself was responsible for placing the CCC camps in Guernsey. I'm not sure if that qualifies him as the parks first visitor, since he only visualized it on paper, but interesting to note he most likely looked at a Wyoming map and said something such as, *"Yes right there, Guernsey Lake, let's put a camp or two there."*[63]

The CCC quickly became a popular program both in and outside of Washington. Two months after its inception the first of the two camps at Guernsey was authorized and a year later it was in full operation. By then (1934) the program was a resounding success. News stories across the nation reported economic upturns as a result of money being sent home from young men in the CCC.[64]

Camps nationwide gave out glowing reports of hard working young men and the projects they finished were receiving rave notices. The camps were doing so well that Senators and Representative from every state were lobbying Roosevelt for additional camps in their states. The number of camps was growing fast with many men deciding to serve more than their one, half year, enrollment. To help some of the men for life after the CCC educational and vocational training was added. By 1935 the CCC operated camps for African Americans, Native Indians and Veterans along with the regular young man camps.[65]

With his first re-election coming up Roosevelt was worried about the amount of money being spent on the CCC. He told his closest advisors he was going to cut back to 300,000 men and do away with hundreds of camps.[66] When the idea of cuts became public there was a general outcry of protests. The Civilian Conservation Corps was popular throughout America and citizens were up in arms about the upcoming cuts.

Roosevelt was steadfast about keeping the cuts in place and bringing federal spending under control. He announced the plan would take effect in January of 1936, Company 1858, Camp BR-10, on the west side of Lake Guernsey fell victim to these cuts. The men of BR-10 had completed Skyline Drive, several trails, cleaned up a small beach and picnic area at Davis Bay, and finished the difficult road to Brimmer Point. BR-10 workers were also well on the way to finishing the remarkable picnic shelter on the north ridge that would become known as the Castle.

The east-side men of BR-9 finished the work on the west side. Work started by Camp-10 but finished by Camp-9 included, not only the Castle, but Brimmer Point Lookout. Other projects had been planned for the west side, more trails including equestrian trails, and the possibility of more large work with native limestone, but were never started. Projects were left on paper and on the drawing boards of CCC planners, things that could have been.

Only minimal records are available on the impact the CCC had on the nation's young men. A large percentage of CCC workers had never been out of the state where they were born. Camp BR-9, the first camp in Guernsey, was initially staffed entirely with young men from Texas. Later men from all over the state of Wyoming and the American West would be part of both Guernsey camps. The CCC camps may have made the United States a more mobile nation with young men from all parts of the country moving for CCC work and at times settling in parts of America far from where they grew up.

By 1937 Roosevelt tried, unsuccessfully, to get Congress to make the CCC permanent. Congress did extend the Corps for another two years but the serious talk of a permanent Civilian Conservation Corps died with this last effort.[67] Congress still saw the CCC as a valuable program offering relief in a temporary manor. But not something for long term job training or job growth. At the time this seemed to be a turnaround for congress, during the election year they couldn't live without it, but a year after elections it was another matter. It was the late 1930s and the catchphrase, "politics first, programs second,"[68] seemed to fit solidly in place.

In his second term Roosevelt developed long-term plans for the reorganization of the administration of several departments within his government. Congress was less than thrilled with the idea until early 1939. After floor, and behind closed doors debate, congress authorized the proposal only slightly different than what FDR had asked for. Instead of many offices with many leaders they were grouped together. The CCC, like other departments, was no longer an independent agency.

Civilian Conservation Corps Director Fechner was understandably upset knowing he would now be playing second fiddle in his own CCC. Fechner protested and resigned as director. He later withdrew his resignation, likely at the request of President Roosevelt. This may have been the last straw for Fechner who had been in poor health, but remained on the job anyway. In December his frail condition took a turn for the worse and he died of heart failure on the last day of December.[69]

With Fechner gone the CCC was nearing the end of its run. John McEntee was appointed by Roosevelt to be the new head of the Corps. McEntee did not have the strong, get along, ability of his predecessor and struggled through slightly more than two difficult years of work as the director.[70] By the middle of 1941 war was looming and the number of men signing up was falling off. The CCC once 600,000 strong now was under 200,000.

Public sentiment waned as more and more men were needed for the war effort and jobs were, once again, becoming plentiful in America. The Great Depression was winding down. A few months after the December seventh bombing of Pearl Harbor congress recommended the CCC be abolished by the first of July 1942.[71]

Sadly, World War II moved the tree planters, stone masons, road and trail building men of the CCC from parks and projects to the pages of history books. Unfortunately the history of the CCC garners scarcely a paragraph in today's high school history books. I personally combed through a 2013 edition of a high school United States History textbook, and found 64 words and two, postage stamp size photos with a small caption, and that was it. Nothing else was found. A quick web search of the CCC will yield hundreds of results but not much information, with most sites rehashing the same few paragraphs of information.

The CCC was certainly experimental, and occasionally ran by knee jerk reaction or flying by the seat of their pants planning. But it worked, critics might say, "somehow it worked." Maybe it worked because they never lost focus on the goal - jobs for young men. Projects were decided as new camps were formed. There were no long term goals, no long term studies to determine these goals, only unemployed men finding work and sending money home.

From time to time various work programs are proposed or even tried for a time, most on the state level. None have succeeded, not like the CCC. But then not many governments have come up with a single program that worked as well as the Civilian Conservation Corps.

It's legacy? Look around. Guernsey State Park and many other state and national parks across America started as CCC projects. Cities and counties all over the country still show evidence of the work of the Civilian Conservation Corps.

Looking North from Lower Spotted Tail

Chapter 10 – Before the CCC

To Build a Dam

The Bureau of Reclamation did a considerable amount of work in America's Western states in the early part of the 1900s. From 1905 to the early 1920s, 2,000 miles of canals were built in Western Nebraska and Eastern Wyoming. The idea had long been held that a dam would be built in Goshen County to supply these canals with irrigation water when the need was greatest. At the time of their building they were fed by the river but the constant changing of river levels made this system less than perfect for farmers needing crop water at specific points of the growing season.[72]

The deep canyons of the North Platte River a mile north of Guernsey looked much more promising for building a dam, to the Bureau of Reclamation, than did the flat river area of Goshen County. The Bureau of Reclamation stated several purposes for the Guernsey dam, but most of all, it was to be used for control of water released upstream from Pathfinder reservoir.[73] By 1915 citizens of eastern Wyoming were looking for a place to generate electricity and this dam site just north of Guernsey, was the solution. It could be used to control excessive amounts of snow melt runoff water and supply irrigation water for thousands of Eastern Wyoming and Western Nebraska acres. It would also generate much needed power for citizens of the North Platte River Valley.

Powerplant

Waterfall at the Spillway

Charles A. Guernsey - Legacy

Charles A. Guernsey - photo circa 1930
Photo – Waring Historical Collection – Photo Credit unknown

The story of Guernsey State Park would be incomplete without a mention of Charles Guernsey, the man who both the state park and nearby town are named after. His role in persuading the Bureau of Reclamation to build and place the North Platte River dam in its present location cannot be understated.

From Mr. Guernsey's wonderful book, *Wyoming Cowboy Days,* one paragraph, in quotation marks but not attributed to anyone sums up the long journey of Guernsey in getting the dam built near the town that would be named after him.

"It is an interesting coincidence and a bit of romance interwoven with history that former State Senator Charles A. Guernsey and former State Engineer Elwood Mead, then in his twenties, first selected this very site for a power dam across the Platte River. Nearly forty years later, Elwood Meade, a Commissioner of Reclamation, was able to crystalize Charles Guernsey's dream into mortar and stone. This dam is massive and magnificent and the surrounding's adapt themselves very easily for a beautiful park and playground. A wide causeway for automobiles spans the dam."[74]

The tale of how Mr. Guernsey got the project started sounds more like fiction than the truth. The park was named after the town and Guernsey must have been both highly respected and most influential to have both a city and a state park honoring him.

From the 1840s the area where the town of Guernsey is now located was referred to as the, Emigrants Wash Tub. Warm Springs, situated south of Guernsey not far from the Trail Ruts and the CCC built fish rearing ponds, was the site were emigrants sometimes stopped to wash clothes and bath, thus the Wash Tub moniker.

In 1880 a young New Yorker, Charles A. Guernsey, made his way west. Guernsey became a rancher and later a politician in the Lusk and then Guernsey area. In 1902 the town was incorporated when the, Chicago, Burlington and Quincy Railroad reached the area. Now it needed a name, or at least one better than Wash Tub, Wyoming.

With the railroad and town site in their vision the Hartville Newspaper, the *Iron Gazette*, had already suggested the town be named Guernsey more than two years before it was named.[75]

The headline, "Call It Guernsey,"[76] was all that most readers needed to understand where the only area newspaper stood on the naming of the new, nearby village.

Guernsey was popular in the area because of his early interest and financial backing of the mines in Sunrise, near Hartville. Of Mr. Guernsey the *Iron Gazette* said. "Hon. Charles A. Guernsey, with a courage born of his conviction and belief in the future of the fields, with indomitable perseverance, under the most adverse circumstances, continued developments and extolled the merits of the district."[77]

Sunrise Mine - circa 1890-1900
Photo – Waring Historical Collection – Photo Credit unknown

Charles Guernsey Hijacks a Train

Commandeering a trainload of dignitaries from Washington D.C. may not be the best means of persuasion but in Guernsey's case it worked. It was September of 1909 and a group of 40 men were on a Senate directed mission to look over reclamation projects in the west. Charles Guernsey met the train in Mitchell, Nebraska with hopes of talking the chairman of the group, Senator Thomas H. Carter of Montana, into a small side trip. The following is the story as Guernsey relates it in his book, *"Wyoming Cowboy Days."*[78]

Turn of the Century (1900) Train
Photo – Waring Historical Collection – Photo Credit unknown

When Guernsey boarded the train he walked directly to Senator Carter. Knowing of Carter's repetition for grumpiness, he quickly explained he wanted the train to take a six mile, out of the way, trip to the Sunrise Mines. As briefly as possible Guernsey tried to enlighten the senator as to why the mine could use power created by a dam on the river near Guernsey.

The Senator politely, but a bit irritated, listened to Guernsey's plea for a side trip to see why the Bureau of Reclamation should build a dam on the North Platte River near Guernsey. According to Mr. Guernsey the Senator answered immediately, Senator Carter well known for being to the point, certainly was here, his answer, "No."[79]

Most people would take Carter's answer to mean no, but not Charles Guernsey. He waited until the train reached the town of Guernsey where it was to stop and switch engines. Here he directed the engineer to take the train to Sunrise, and off they went.

When they reached the Sunrise Mine the train stopped and Guernsey invited the large group, of now sour faced dignitaries, to get off and take a look. After much grumbling the group left the train and were amazed by the site of 300 workers mining the bright red hematite ore from the glory hole at Sunrise.

The grumbling was soon forgotten and exchanged for happy claps on the back from the hijacked passengers. Senator Carter was so excited he asked Mr. Guernsey to ride the train back to Cheyenne as a guest of the group. Guernsey had planned to leave the train after it made the six mile trip back to the stationhouse in town but changed his mind. Mr. Guernsey felt the least he could do would be to ride the train he had hijacked or misdirected along with his former detainees. This single incident was not the reason the Bureau of

Reclamation built the dam, but it certainly helped get the project known and the process started. [80]

Guernsey Dam Today – Photo from Roundtop Mountain

Cost to Build the Dam

Planning the dam at Guernsey took the Bureau of Reclamation several years and when it was ready the project stayed a blue print for nearly ten years. At long last the sixty-eighth Congress of the United States allocated $800,000 for the construction.[81] The bill was passed December 5, 1924 and the works were in place for construction. Utah Construction from Salt Lake City was the only bidder. Their bid of $ 1,200,000 dollars was accepted and signed in early May of 1925.[82] By late May the company was at work. The work was started and the additional $400,000 needed was picked up by the Bureau until congress appropriated more money for the completion of the dam latter on in the session. By the time the dam was complete the cost ran to 2,344,000.[83]

Construction

Construction started with workers living in a temporary tent camp which soon grew to a group of more than 30 buildings including cottages, bunk houses, a mess hall, bath house/recreation hall, offices and a warehouse. By summer more than 200 men were working. The work, done with steam shovels and plenty of hand work, was hard and dangerous. In August the company lost their first man, killed in a rock slide.[84]

The crews, along with the steam shovels, used trucks, small bulldozers and the railroad to move, remove, and replace rock. The dam itself was formed of sluiced clay, sand, gravel, dirt and rock fill. The material was mixed to the proportions needed then hauled by rail-cars and dumped at the dam site. A large portion of the middle of the dam is clay extending to thirty feet below the bottom of the original river bed. To finish the dam a three foot deep layer of rock riprap was spread over the face. This step might not be much today but in 1926-27 this was done by hand. A time consuming task of one or two rocks, carried and placed by hand, by dozens of workers. At the bottom and top of the dam small wheelbarrows allowed workers to carry a few more rocks but only a small part of the labor days were spent working on the bottom and top of the dam.[85]

Limestone and dolomite rock were spread toward the top to keep constant wave action from wearing down that part of the dam. The crest of the dam was reinforced with a concrete wall, three feet high, on the lake side of the dam. In 2013-14 when the dam was being rebuilt and reinforced, additional height was added to the wall. The downstream side of the dam has a short wall with a protective chain link fence attached.

Dam during the 2013 Rebuild of the Gates

Guernsey dam has held water and worked well with no record of major leaks or breaks over nearly a century. The recent rebuilding of the gates was only preventive. During the rebuild work was done on the gates to insure their performance for many more years. Like the first gates they are built to last into the next century.

The dam itself stands 135 feet high and 560 feet long and contains more than half a million cubic yards of fill material. The normal water pool at the dam face is 92 feet deep. The dam has a drainage area of nearly 2,150 square miles. Construction was completed July 13, 1927 with the power-plant starting generation activities two days later.[86]

In more modern times it is hard to understand the amount of hand work it took to build and back fill a dam of this size. The men had a few small trucks and a rail line was built to haul heavy materials, the rest was done by Utah Construction Company workers with wheelbarrows, picks, shovels, sweat and blisters. Truly a magnificent undertaking and a tribute to their abilities and work ethics.

Below the Dam - Water being released through the Gatehouse

In 1927 the full dam could support 72,000 acre feet of water but today after many years of silt, it holds only about two-thirds of the water the original held with a full pool of 46,000 acres. After reworking of the dams gates from March of 2013 to May of 2014 the lake was brought to a high water level never before seen.

Flooded Day Use Area during High Water

This new high water mark looked, to the untrained eye, to have brought the pool back well over 50,000 acre feet and possibly closer to 55,000 acre feet of water. Soon after the high water test the pool was reduced to more, modern time, normal levels.

The Gatehouse

One of the dam's focal points, the north spillway gatehouse, is like nothing else in the park. The park features so much of the magnificent Civilian Conservation Corps rustic building that the gatehouse seems out of place with its classic arches.

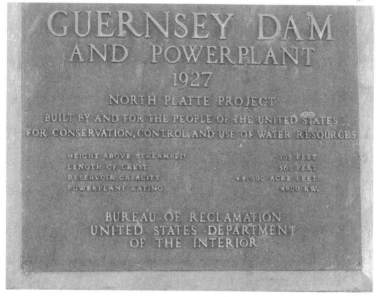

Gatehouse Plaque

The gatehouse raises and lowers a 50 foot square, 434,000 pound head gate. The ironclad gate, filled with a mixture of heavy concrete and native stone from the park, was built especially for the Guernsey, North Platte River dam. A one of a kind, Guernsey Dam gate.

Gatehouse

Morning Glory Spillway

The south, Morning Glory Spillway, is 128 feet long and was controlled by two 64 by 14 and a half foot drum gates until 2014.[87]

The 2013-14 rebuild and work on the dam closed one of the two original south gates after 86 years of service. Now one, newly rebuilt, gate controls the south side spillway.

The power plant, supplied with water through a south side gate has two 2,400 kilowatt generators and has been sending power to downstream users since 1927. During low water times the majority of water released downstream travels through the Powerplant.

In 1981, Guernsey Dam, the Powerplant and the Gatehouse were placed on the National Register of Historic Places. While much of the park stands as a salute to the Civilian Conservation Corps, the Dam itself, the Power-plant and Gatehouse reflect the remarkable work of the Bureau of Reclamation, a decade before the CCC, 1925-1927.

Road across Guernsey Dam shortly after CCC men finished curbing and lights
Photo – Waring Historical Collection – Photo Credit unknown

The south dam-gates and part of the dam itself was under re-construction for the entire year of 2013, the project started in January with completion in June of 2014.

Turning Two Gates into One in 2013

This work on rebuilding the gates was the first substantial work on the dam since its building in the 1920s. The gates are the most important part of a working dam and in one as large as Guernsey they must work flawlessly. When full, water is backed up for 13 miles, the reservoir covers an area of 2375 acres, which is slightly over a quarter of the park. With drought dominating the climate over the past three decades the dam has pooled less water than normal many years. But in the summer of construction in 2013 the water was kept at its lowest levels since the dam was built. By May the dam was raised to an all-time high water mark. Water sports enthusiasts and park visitors were heartened to see the dam full, once again, for the summer of 2014.

Full Lake - summer 2014

Chapter 11 – The Modern Park

Guernsey State Park Today

Today the Park at Guernsey stands as a lasting tribute to the Civilian Conservation Corps and to the hard working men of Camp number 844, BR-9 on the east side of the park and to Camp 1858, BR-10 on the west side. Guernsey State Park now hosts visitors numbering in the tens of thousands each year.

The CCC was active in Wyoming with 18 camps, some grew and were expanded with additional men into sub camps or spike camps as outreaches from the regular camp. But of all the camps only two were involved in, or were part of, the development of a state park. The two camps at Guernsey were the park builders, together they did an enormous amount of work shaping a North Platte River reservoir into an Eastern Wyoming treasure, the picturesque and functional Guernsey State Park.[88]

Over the years new campgrounds have been added, roads and trails have been expanded and others eliminated. Indeed, two of the most popular camping and recreational areas in the park were added after CCC activities in the park were long past. These two areas, Long Canyon and Sandy Beach, added many camping areas, additional restrooms and two boat ramps to the park.

Sandy Beach

Camping remains one of the most popular activities in the park, and now the modern convenience of fresh water stations, handicap camp sites, and electric hookups make camping comfortable for everyone. As visitors enter the park from the south road a modern dump station is available for campers.

Newest additions to the park are four European style Yurts on the parks west side and coin operated showers near the park headquarters on the east side. The park is also making upgrades to the campground water systems and building additional tent and handicap sites throughout the park.

One of the Skyline Drive Yurts

The Yurts are located on the west side of Skyline Drive between Davis Bay and the Castle. They are available for daily rental and are fully handicap assessable. The park continues to evolve and now features seven campgrounds with multiple camp sites in each, three boat launching ramps, restrooms, picnic shelters and fresh water supply stations throughout the park.[89] Mountain biking, and rock climbing have joined water sports, hiking and picnicking as some of the most enjoyed activities in the park. The forested mountain sides and grassy valleys make the park a wildlife and bird watchers paradise and perfect for photographers.

Wild Turkey are found on both sides of the lake

A large number of Mule Deer live in the Park

Although seldom seen, Pronghorn are found in the western and northern extremes of the park. Black bears are infrequent park visitors. A variety of snakes, including prairie rattlesnakes, along with bobcats and small animals of all kinds thrive in the park. A mountain lion or two may live in or pass through the parks more than 8,000 acres as they are in the area.

Moose and Elk, not reportedly seen in the park, do live in the area and on occasion might slip in for a visit to the park.

The park is also the home of many large birds, both waterfowl and birds of prey, with Bald Eagles and several types of hawks living in the park. It is also home to a large group of Vultures, well known for being as ugly on the ground as they are beautiful in the air.

Egret below the Dam

**Vultures on the Roost
& In the Air**

Bald Eagles are found throughout the park and are always spectacular

Chapter 12 – End of the Story

Conclusion

The partnership combination of the Bureau of Reclamation and The National Park Service, along with the state of Wyoming's need to develop a state park system, could not possibly have worked out better than it did with the creation of Guernsey State Park.

Visiting the Museum, standing on the Castles overlook, or wandering among the remains of old Camp BR-10, one cannot help but marvel about the men who once lived and worked here as part of the Civilian Conservation Corps. America has long been a country of disposables. Buildings, roads and places are built, used for their intended purposes, then forgotten, torn down or left to ruin. Once in a while something is built that is worth saving, preserving for future generations. Guernsey State Park and the CCC's work in the park is one of those places. An area to come and see what the men of the Civilian Conservation Corps built and a chance to walk where they walked. A rare opportunity to feel how history was made.

Throughout America are places where the work of the CCC has already been lost and more places are deteriorating to a point of fix or replace. Guernsey State Park has preserved much of the great work here in the park. But as with all things, there is work to be done. Two fine examples of CCC bridge work in the park have been severely damaged by fire. These bridges on Tunnel Mountain Trail and Brimmer Point Trail still have the magnificent stonework, solid and in place, but are no longer usable after all decking and rails burned away. The log and wood parts of the bridges will be rebuilt, a big and certainly expensive project, but one that will be undertaken.

The golf course on the parks eastern boundary is another worthwhile reconstruction project. Cost would be minimal to rebuild the small tee boxes and redo the old sand greens. I was unable, in my research, to find any CCC course that has not been drastically remodeled. Many of the Corps built courses have no resemblance today to the original CCC course and design. Most are now heavily irrigated grass green courses where a huge majority of the golfers have no idea the original architect and builder was the Civilian Conservation Corps.

In a few more years it may become impossible to find enough of the original Guernsey Lake Course to rebuild. This project would be terrific for Civilian Conservation Corps history all over the country.

The third and final project that would help preserve the memory of the CCC in the park would be to continue to upgrade the older lost trails. There are trails worth rebuilding on each side of the park. The trails that would be most interesting, if re-marked for users, on the east would be the Onyx Cave road trail, although the CCC did little on this trail, and the Black Canyon trail. On the west side a trail to, and around, the rock quarry, following the old CCC road would be of special interest to history and rock buffs alike.

It would also be wonderful if the old trailhead road and parking lot, between Marsh Mountain and Echo Cave Trail, were made, once again, usable and available to drive vehicles in and park.

The workers and leaders of Guernsey State Park and the Department of State Parks and Cultural Resources have done a nice job of upgrading facilities at Guernsey State Park over the decades since the New Deal. In the past few years more handicap accessibility has been added along with more areas for tent camping. Roads have been upgraded and maintained to allow for the increase in visitors each year. Additional restrooms and play areas for children also make the park more attractive for families.

The CCC Worker Statue

On October 11, 2009 a CCC statue, The CCC Worker Statue-number 53, was dedicated. The statue, of which there are now 61 in 38 different states, stands in front of the Museum. The statue was a project of the Friends of Guernsey State Park and stands as a fitting tribute to CCC workers everywhere. As all too often happens in Wyoming the dedication ceremonies had to be postponed due to heavy snowfall. The wry smile on the statue workers face shows he likely knew something about fickle Wyoming weather.

The CCC Worker Statue, is prominently and proudly displayed on the front cover of this book as a reminder to each who passes by of a time that should not be forgotten.

Trees, the Lake, Laramie Peak and the CCC Worker Statue

Guernsey state park stands as the crown jewel of the Wyoming Parks system. Recreation and history combine with the sheer beauty of Lake Guernsey's North Platte River Canyon, making a park that has stood the test of time and will live on for many more years.

Chapter 13 – Fun in the Park

A Dozen Great Things to do in the Park

The majority of people using Guernsey State Park come for one of two reasons, water sports or camping. The lake and the immediate area surrounding it are set up for those two activities which have been enjoyed by thousands of people for decades. The state park, the community of Guernsey and the state of Wyoming appreciate and enjoy those visitors each year.

Water sports enthusiasts and campers come back year after year to spend time in the park. Long lasting appreciation of the park and lasting friendships are only a few of the rewards benefitting repeat visitors over the years. Many of these visitors continue to expand their park experience by exploring other parts of the park and trying new park activities each year.

It seems unfair to make a list of top things to do or see when visiting the park. With that in mind, and a reminder to readers, these are only a few of the possibilities for educational and recreational activities in Guernsey State Park, here is my list of a dozen things to do in the park, presented in no particular order of interest.

As you travel around and enjoy the park take the time to make some memories of your own favorite, Guernsey State Park places or activities.

Good Luck and enjoy!

Visit the Guernsey State Park Museum – Park your vehicle in the lower area and walk up the CCC rock stairway to the Museum, it is less than a city block and provides both cardio and educational training on the way.

Take a good look at the building itself, both inside and out. Although the displays do an excellent job of presenting local and CCC history it is the building itself that is the greatest display. A demonstration of exquisite workmanship and Rustic Architecture.

Museum looking north from the Upper Parking Lot

Eat lunch in the Sitting Bull Shelter – If you don't have time to lunch in this massive picnic shelter stay long enough to enjoy the view and take some photos. If you move down the hill to the east or south of the shelter a fine view is afforded of how the building seems to grow from the ground, a feature of this type of rustic park architecture.

The Lake View from Sitting Bull

Sitting Bull is a day use only area and is enjoyed by both vacationers and townspeople alike.

Many years ago people may have said of this area," come sit a spell and enjoy." Give it a try!

Enjoy the view from the North Bluff Castle – This is the last of the parks many Rustic Architecture buildings I will steer you toward, but one that shouldn't be missed. The viewing area, reached by winding up a stone stairway affords a magnificent view for miles to the north and west. Part of the reason the Castle Picnic Shelter was built on the North Bluff of the park was because of the, photographers dream, view of Laramie Peak to the west.

View from the North Bluff Castle

Time for a restroom break? Even if it's not break time, walk down to the Million Dollar Biffy, a massive yet somehow whimsical CCC comfort station. This is not one of the dozen list of things to do in the park. Instead it is included here as part of the trip to the Castle on the North Bluff.

The Million Dollar Biffy

Sandy Beach – Take your shoes off and walk along the fine North Platte River Sand. The beach is more than a mile long with many public access points. A leisurely walk along Sandy Beach will lighten your heart and the wandering waters of the river will give you a glimpse into times long past.

Tourists test the water at Sandy Beach

The lake drop off is quite gentle along the beach allowing people using this area to wade out into the water without fear of sudden drop-offs. This is a heavy boating area, so it is best to stay in shallow water.

West Side Trails - Ride or walk at least one – Stop at the sign where Skyline Drive branches onto Brimmer Point Road and read the sign. Several miles of walking and mountain bike trails are shown, try one or ride them all.

Marsh Mountain Trail

The trails range from short to long but all will test peddling abilities. No bicycle, no problem, these are also great hiking trails.

Distance for each trail is marked on the sign and range from less than a mile to several miles if one choses to tie several together, something many bicycle enthusiasts enjoy.

Red Cliff Trail –This is the one trail every visitor needs to try. The Red Cliff Trail starts only one hundred yards west of the dam. After crossing the dam and turning left look for the rustic CCC state park sign on the north side of the road. Steps going up the hill to the trail will be just before reaching this sign and are well marked but still hard to see. This trail is the best example of a CCC engineered and built trail in the park. It also affords spectacular views of the spillway, Powerplant and river below the dam. The steps on this trail are something out of a wonderland, a most magical looking and feeling area.

CCC Steps on the Red Cliff Trail

Stay a night in a Yurt –Not sure what a yurt is? The ones in the park are permanent, but the original Asian yurts were designed to be taken apart and carried on the backs of camels or yaks to the next camping area. We are fresh out of camels and yaks here in Wyoming so these yurts stay in one, handicap assessable, campsite.

Yurts can be rented by the day and are located in a dedicated, Yurts only, campsite on a beautiful bluff, west off Skyline Drive. The Yurts and this camping area were not part of the CCC work in the park but are a wonderful modern day addition.

One of the Yurts on Skyline Drive

Register Cliff and the Ruts – Not part of the park? Yes they are, or at least managed by the park.

Register Cliff is three miles south of Guernsey and well worth a visit. Many pioneer names, carved deeply into the cliff, are still readable today. Register Cliff has a walk trail that takes visitors past well preserved names carved by the pioneers on their way west.

Feel the spirit of the pioneers going west on the Oregon Trail. The ruts at Guernsey are the best remaining signs of the trail in America, several feet deep in places. The Ruts are located one half mile south and one quarter mile west of Guernsey. *(Traveling down main-street Guernsey - Turn right, west, after crossing the river bridge and follow signage)*

Register Cliff

Trail Ruts

While visiting the Ruts the road passes just north of the CCC Fish Rearing Station, now overgrown and long since abandoned.

Brimmer Point – For early risers, the sunrise from the point is out of this world. One of those, I am glad to be alive, sunrises. Not a morning person? Drive up to the point and watch the sunset, spectacular. Or simply take a drive up in the middle of the day, walk the steps up the tower and enjoy the view.

Sunset from Brimmer Point

Not many people turn around and look west from the point, but the view, at sundown, of Laramie Peak through the burned trees is a thing of beauty. Views in every direction are special from the point, the very reason the long winding road and Brimmer Point were placed here by the CCC.

The Powderhouses on Lakeshore Drive – From an historians point of view, no visit to the park would be complete without a visit to the two powderhouses and the tiny cap-house on the east side drive through the park.

The main and well preserved powderhouse is only a few feet off of Lakeshore Drive. An additional powderhouse is located off the drive and cannot be seen from the road. It is located approximately 200 yards northwest of the powderhouse on Lakeshore Drive with the tiny cap-house nearby.

Much more of a rustic look to this Powderhouse located in the trees off Lakeshore Drive

The sounds of the CCC – This is a must for history buffs and little known to most park visitors. On the west side of the lake are the remains of old camp BR-10.

Camp-10 Latrine/Shower House remains

Left behind are the floors of the old buildings along with walkways, roads and the latrine. You can almost hear the men working, talking and enjoying camp life. Perhaps you will hear them if you listen intently and if you fold yourself into the dreams and work of the Civilian Conservation Corps camp.

Drive Lakeshore or Skyline – When park visitors are lacking for time or visiting the park for only a quick look, I would suggest one of the CCC drives, Lakeshore on the east side or Skyline on the west side. Enjoy the beauty of the natural settings, you'll be back. My wife and I travel these two drives more than 100 times each year and still look forward to every trip.

View along Lakeshore Drive

Wildlife Watching in the Park

Mule Deer and Wild Turkey

Cottontail and early spring Robin

Mallards leaving and a Woodpecker at work

Canadian Geese on Ice and a Merganser on the water

Blue Jay and a Mule Deer Doe

Cormorants and a pair of Great Blue Herons

Cedar Waxwing and American Bald Eagle

Chapter 14 – Park Land

Chronology of Events - Guernsey State Park

70-40, Million Years Ago - The North Platte River was created after intense plate tectonic activity took place roughly 70-40 million years ago forming the Rocky Mountains and the North Platte, along with hundreds of other rivers and streams. The drainage starts at the Continental Divide digging the shallow Platte, for over 700 miles. The river path varied by the amount of soft soil, gravel and rock it had to traverse.

1811, Trails West - The Oregon and Mormon Trails, following closely the path of the river, pass on either side of the park and south of the town of Guernsey. Wilson Price Hunt is credited with finding the route the trails would take. His first crossing was as the leader of an expedition traveling overland back to Missouri. Hunt headed up the Astor Expedition, returning from a trip to the Columbia River where they established Fort Astoria. No wagons yet traveled the trail as early as 1811, but the trappers and Mountain Men were blazing this trail by that time.

1836 - The first wagon train heads west with a destination of Fort Hall, in present day Idaho.

1846-1869 - Busy time along the trails west with reportedly more than 400,000 people going west.

1905 - Irrigation canals started - First Irrigation canals were built using water from the North Platte River. The water diversions started downstream from Guernsey with Goshen County in Wyoming and several Western Nebraska counties benefitting. From 1905 to the early 1920s over 2,000 miles of canals were completed.

September, 1909 – Charles Guernsey detours train of Washington D.C. dignitaries to the Sunrise Mine.

May 20, 1924 – President Coolidge recommends that $800,000 be set aside for, "continued investigation and commencement of the Guernsey reservoir and incidental operation."[90]

December 5, 1924 - Congress passes bill funding Guernsey Dam construction

May, 1925 - Construction started on the dam under the supervision of the United States Bureau of Reclamation

July 13, 1927 – Construction of dam completed

May 21, 1934 - Civilian Conservation Corps, Camp RS-1 is built on the east side below the Museum. Camp RS-1, the first, Civilian Conservation Corps Reclamation Camp, soon became Camp BR-9 working on the first North Platte River Project in Wyoming. The camp was established, during the third enrolment period for workers.

July 6, 1934 - A second CCC camp, opened at Guernsey Lake State Park. This second camp would initially be occupied by the men of Company No.1858 and would become Camp BR-10, to be built on the west side, west of Mae West Hill

August, 1938 – The Civilian Conservation Corps is moved out of Guernsey

June, 1942 – The CCC ends in America with a narrow vote in congress to eliminate funding. Eight Million dollars was appropriated to liquidate the corps.

August 26, 1980 – The Powerplant Building, Dam and Gatehouse (the north gate with the spectacular spillway) added to the National Historic Landmark Register.

September 25, 1997 - Lake Guernsey State Park designated a National Historic Landmark. The two designations, 1980 and 1997 now had designated everything built by the Bureau of Reclamation and Civilian Conservation Corps at Guernsey Lake State Park on the National Historic Landmark registrar.

Summer, 2012 – Fire burns through areas on both sides of the reservoir destroying hundreds of years of nature's work and historically valuable CCC bridges and trails

January, 2013- April 2014- The portion of Lakeshore Drive, crossing the dam, closed while dam and spillways are under reconstruction.

April, 2015 – Publication of - *The CCC & the Building of Guernsey State park – With Stories and Folktales of the Park.*

End Notes from Preface

*William W. Savage Jr., *Cowboy Life: Reconstructing an American Myth* (University Press of Colorado, 1975),

*Owen Wister, *The Virginian: A Horseman of the Plains* (Macmillan, 1902) Intro IX

End Notes

[1] From many sources including, Gerhard Peters and John T. Woolley, *The American Presidency Project, Roosevelt,* online edition *2013*

[2] J. H. Coffman, *Record of Work and Accomplishments of CCC enrollees in Camp BR-9, Wyoming* (Wyoming State Parks & Historic Sites Digital Collections – Guernsey Museum Digitization Project) Tabulations of Main Developments, 1

[3] Civilian Conservation Corps Legacy, *CCC Camps   Wyoming,*   1 www.ccclegacy.org/ccc.camps.wyoming.htr

[4] Information taken from CCC Worker Statue Plaque at the Guernsey State Park Museum

[5] Boston Evening Transcript, January 3, 1935 & November 2, 1936

[6] Christine Pfaff, *Bureau of Reclamation Civilian Conservation Corps Study,* (Bureau of Reclamation, Denver, 2009), A-55

[7] Christine Pfaff, *Bureau of Reclamation Civilian Conservation Corps Study*, A-55

[8] J. H. Coffman, *Record of Work and Accomplishments of CCC enrollees in Camp BR-9, Wyoming* (Wyoming State Parks & Historic Sites Digital Collections – Guernsey Museum Digitization Project) Tabulations of Main Developments, 1

[9] John A. Salmond, *The Civilian Conservation Corps 1933-1942,* (Duke University Press, Durham North Carolina 1967) 120

[10] Ibid

[11] R.G Redell, *Master Plan Report for Lake Guernsey Park,* Revised September 1, 1937, 7B

[12] Neil Waring, Wyoming History Teaching Notes, Unpublished and unnumbered, 1970-2012

[13] Ibid

[14] Ibid

[15] Ibid

[16] Ibid

[17]Mountain Project, http://www.mountainproject.com/v/area-3-the-revolutionary-climbing-wall-of-dead-mans gulch/107461853

[18] R.G Redell, *Master Plan Report for Lake Guernsey Park,* Revised September 1, 1937, 7B

[19] Jones – Redell, Department of Interior, National Park Service, North Platte Project, Bureau of Reclamation Co-op, *(Revised Master Plan, Region VI Wyoming BR-9 BR-10),* **Map D**, September 1, 1937

[20]   Jones – Redell, Department of Interior, National Park Service, North Platte Project, Bureau of Reclamation Co-op, **Map F**

[21]   Anthony M. Belli, *Lost Treasure, Slade's Long Lost Loot,* (January, 2000), 27

[22]   Mark Twain, *Roughing It,* (American Publishing Company 1872), 79

[23]   Mark Twain, *Roughing It,* (American Publishing Company 1872), 79

[24] Plaque at the Museum

[25] Wyoming State Parks and Historic Sites, *Guernsey Museum Digitization Project,* http://wyoshpo.state.wy.us/westerntrails/stateparks.html

[26] National Park Service Rustic Architecture, *Roosevelt's Emergency Programs 1933-1935, 1-10* http://www.cr.nps.gov/history/online_books/rusticarch/
introduction.htm

[27]   Christine Pfaff, *Bureau of Reclamation Civilian Conservation Corps Study,* (Bureau of Reclamation, Denver, 2009), A-57

[28]   Christine Pfaff, *Bureau of Reclamation Civilian Conservation Corps Study,* A-55

[29]   Wyoming State Parks and Historic Sites, *Guernsey Museum Digitization Project,* (REDCCC Photo 20 SPHS – see caption) http://wyoshpo.state.wy.us/westerntrails/stateparks.html

[30] Jones – Redell, Department of Interior, National Park Service, North Platte Project, Bureau of Reclamation Co-op, *(Sixth Period Development*

Plan, Region VI Wyoming BR-9 BR-10), **Map A**, August 22, 1935

[31] Jones – Redell, Department of Interior, National Park Service, North Platte Project, Bureau of Reclamation Co-op, *(Sixth Period Development Plan, Region VI Wyoming BR-9 BR-10)*, **Map A**, August 22, 1935

-Also-

North Platte Irrigation Project and Recreational Area Wyoming, *Map 40-95*, 1940

[32] R. G. Redell, Guernsey Lake Master Plan Report, *Developments of Lake View Camp DBR 10-W,* **Map B**, September 1, 1937

[33] J. H. Coffman, *Record of Work and Accomplishments of CCC enrollees in Camp BR-9, Wyoming* (Wyoming State Parks & Historic Sites Digital Collections – Guernsey Museum Digitization Project) Tabulations of Main Developments, 7 - (Notes are not dated but were written between the closing of BR-10 in January of 1936 and closing of BR-9 in August of 1938. The North Bluff Castle was planned and mostly built by camp BR-10 but finished by Camp BR-9)

[34] Boles Blogs, *http://bolesblogs,com*

[35] Ken Druce, For Boles Blogs, *The Guernsey Lake Castle, March 11, 2001, http://bolesblogs,com*

[36] North Platte Irrigation Project and Recreational Area Wyoming, *Map 40-95*, 1940

[37] Jim Snyder, Unpublished Notes with Bureau of Reclamation Maps, Guernsey Wyoming 1991

38 Christine Pfaff, *Bureau of Reclamation Civilian Conservation Corps Study,* (Bureau of Reclamation, Denver, 2009), A-56

39 Stan Cohen, The Tree Army – *A Pictorial History of the Civilian Conservation Corps, 1933-1942* (Pictorial Histories Publishing Company, Missoula Montana, 1980), 7

40 Gerald W. Williams, *The Civilian Conservation Corps and National Forests – Looking Back Forest Service History,* March, 21, 2008, 4

41 Christine Pfaff, *Bureau of Reclamation Civilian Conservation Corps Study,* (Bureau of Reclamation, Denver, 2009), A-57

42 J. H. Coffman, *Record of Work and Accomplishments of CCC enrollees in Camp BR-9, Wyoming* (Wyoming State Parks & Historic Sites Digital Collections – Guernsey Museum Digitization Project) Tabulations of Main Developments, 6

43 Ibid

44 R. G. Redell, Guernsey Lake Master Plan Report, *Developments of Lake View Camp DBR 10-W,* **Map B**, September 1, 1937

45 Ibid

46 Gaylord Miller from J. H. Coffman, *General History Lake Guernsey Park, Camp BR-9, Wyoming* (Wyoming State Parks & Historic Sites Digital Collections – Guernsey Museum Digitization Project) Tabulations of Main Developments, 5

47 J. H. Coffman, *Record of Work and Accomplishments of CCC enrollees in Camp BR-9, Wyoming* (Wyoming State Parks & Historic Sites Digital Collections – Guernsey Museum Digitization Project) Tabulations of Main Developments, 8

[48] Ibid, 7-8

[49] Jim Snyder, Unpublished notes attached to Trail Map E, 1991

[50] Jones – Redell, Department of Interior, National Park Service, North Platte Project, Bureau of Reclamation Co-op, Planting, **Map E**

[51] Jim Snyder, Unpublished notes attached to Trail Map E, 1991

[52] Ibid

[53] James F. Justin, *Civilian Conservation Corps Facts – Lest We Forget,* Civilian Conservation Corps Museum, http://www.justinMuseum.com/famjustin/ccchis.html

[54] John A. Salmond, *The Civilian Conservation Corps 1933-1942,* (Duke University Press, Durham North Carolina 1967) 129

[55] Neil Waring, unpublished work, *42 Years In Front of the Class,* From Waring notes 1993

[56] Torrington Telegram, July 19, 1934

[57] J. H. Coffman, *Record of Work and Accomplishments of CCC enrollees in Camp BR-9, Wyoming* (Wyoming State Parks & Historic Sites Digital Collections – Guernsey Museum Digitization Project) Introduction, 1

[58] Wyoming State Parks & Historic Sites Digital Collections – Guernsey Museum Digitization Project, 2. Notes are not dated but were written between the closing of BR-10 in January of 1936 and closing of BR-9 in August of 1938.

[59] National Park Service, Form-10-900 Guernsey State Park

[60] Park Net - National Park Service, *Parkitecture In Western National Parks, Early Twentieth Century Rustic Design & Naturalism,* *http://www.nps.gov/hdp/exhibits/parkitect*

[61] Stan Cohen, The Tree Army – *A Pictorial History of the Civilian Conservation Corps, 1933-1942* (Pictorial Histories Publishing Company, Missoula Montana, 1980), 6,7

[62] Ibid, 7

[63] Neil Waring, *words of the author, certainly not the words of Mr. Roosevelt,* from the authors unpublished work, *42 Years In Front of the Class,* From Waring notes 1993

[64] Civilian Conservation Corps Legacy, *Passing the Legacy To Future Generations,* CCC a Brief History – The Program Had Great Support http://www.ccclegacy.org/CCC_Brief_History.html

[65] Bill Gonzel - Gonzel Group, *Wessels Living History Farm, Farming in the 1930s* http://www.livinghistoryfarm.org/farminginthe30s/farminginthe1930s.html

[66] Civilian Conservation Corps Legacy http://www.ccclegacy.org/CCC_Brief_History.html

[67] Stan Cohen, The Tree Army – *A Pictorial History of the Civilian Conservation Corps, 1933-1942* (Pictorial Histories Publishing Company, Missoula Montana, 1980), 145

[68] Neil Waring, unpublished work, *42 Years In Front of the Class,* From Waring notes 1993

[69] John A. Salmond, *The Civilian Conservation Corps 1933-1942,* (Duke University Press, Durham North Carolina 1967) 170-176

[70] Ibid, 213-217

[71] Stan Cohen, The Tree Army, 145

[72] Autobee Robert, *North Platte Project, Bureau of Reclamation, 1996, 40*

[73] Ibid

[74] Charles H. Guernsey, *Wyoming Cowboy Days, G.P. Putnam's Sons, New York, 1936, 236*

[75] Iron Gazette, Hartville Wyoming, Volume 1, Number 1, November 17, 1899

[76] Ibid

[77] Ibid

[78] Charles H. Guernsey, *Wyoming Cowboy Days, G.P. Putnam's Sons, New York, 1936, 237-241*

[79] Ibid

[80] Ibid

[81] Robert Autobee *North Platte Project, Bureau of Reclamation, 1996, 21*

[82] Ibid, 23

[83] Charles H. Guernsey, *Wyoming Cowboy Days, G.P. Putnam's Sons, New York, 1936, 248*

[84] Ibid

[85] Robert Autobee *North Platte Project, Bureau of Reclamation, 1996, 23-24*

[86] National Park Service U.S Department of Interior Bureau of Reclamation, Historic Dams and Water Projects-*Managing Water in the West-Guernsey Dam-Wyoming* http://www.nps.gov/nr/travel/ReclamationDamsAndWaterProjects/Guernsey_Dam.html

[87] Reclamation – Managing Water in the West Guernsey Dam South Spillway Hydraulic Model Study, summary,6-10

http://www.usbr.gov/pmts/hydraulics_lab/pubs/
HL/HL-2012-04.pdf

[88] Civilian Conservation Corps Legacy
http://www.ccclegacy.org

[89] Wyoming State Parks and Historic Sites
Guernsey State Park, http://wyoparks.state.wy.us

[90] Charles H. Guernsey, 234

Sources – Bibliography

Books

Cohen, Stan, The Tree Army – *A Pictorial History of the Civilian Conservation Corps, 1933-1942* (Pictorial Histories Publishing Company, Missoula Montana, 1980)

Cornebise, Alfred Emile, *The CCC Chronicles*, Camp Newspapers of the Civilian Conservation Corps, 1933-1942, McFarland, 2004

Guernsey, Charles H., *Wyoming Cowboy Days, G.P. Putnam's Sons, New York, 1936*

Leake, Fred E. and Carter, Ray S., *Roosevelt's Tree Army A Brief History of the Civilian Conservation Corps*, Sixth Edition 1987 edited by Richard A. Long and John C. Bigbee, (pamphlet)

Salmond, John A. *The Civilian Conservation Corps 1933-1942,* (Duke University Press, Durham North Carolina 1967)

Savage, William W. Jr., *Cowboy Life: Reconstructing an American Myth,* University Press of Colorado, 1975

The Civilian Conservation Corps, 1933-1942, Duke University Press, Durham, North Carolina 1967 ------5

Twain, Mark, *Roughing It,* American Publishing Company, 1872

Wister, Owen, *The Virginian: A Horseman of the Plains,* Macmillan, 1902

WPA Writers, *Wyoming: A Guide to Its History, Highways, and People,* a project book, University of Nebraska Press reprint of the 1941 addition, Oxford University Press, New York, 1981

Government Documents

Autobee, Robert, *North Platte Project, Bureau of Reclamation, 1996*

Coffman, J. H. *Record of Work and Accomplishments of CCC enrollees in Camp BR-9, Wyoming* (Wyoming State Parks & Historic Sites Digital Collections – Guernsey Museum Digitization Project) Tabulations of Main Developments (Notes are not dated but were written between the closing of BR-10 in January of 1936 and closing of BR-9 in August of 1938. The North Bluff Castle was planned and mostly built by camp BR-10 but finished by Camp BR-9)

Dow, James R., Welsch, Roger L., and Dow, Susan D., Editors, *Wyoming Folklore,* Collected By the

Federal Writers Project, University of Nebraska Press, 2010

Jones – Redell, R. G., Department of Interior, National Park Service, North Platte Project, Bureau of Reclamation Co-op, *Revised Master Plan, Region VI Wyoming BR-9 & BR-10,* September 1, 1937

Miller, Gaylord from J. H. Coffman notes, *General History Lake Guernsey Park, Camp BR-9, Wyoming,* Wyoming State Parks & Historic Sites Digital Collections, Guernsey Museum Digitization Project, Tabulations of Main Developments

National Park Service U.S Department of Interior Bureu of Reclamation, Historic Dams and Water Projects-*Managing Water in the West - Guernsey Dam Wyoming*
http://www.nps.gov/nr/travel/ReclamationDamsAndWaterProjects/Guernsey_Dam.html

National Park Service, Form-10-900 Guernsey State Park

North Platte Irrigation Project and Recreational Area Wyoming, Map *40-95,* 1940

Pfaff, Christine, *Bureau of Reclamation Civilian Conservation Corps Study,* Bureau of Reclamation, Denver, 2009

R.G Redell, *Master Plan Report for Lake Guernsey Park,* Revised September 1, 1937

Reclamation – Managing Water in the West, *Guernsey Dam South Spillway Hydraulic Model Study,* summary 6-10

Redell, R.G, *Master Plan Report for Lake Guernsey Park,* Revised September 1, 1937
U.S. Department of Interior, Bureau of Reclamation, *Annual Project History, North Platte Project,* Vol. 13, 1925

U.S. Department of Interior, Bureau of Reclamation, *Annual Project History, North Platte Project,* Vol. 14, 1926

U.S. Department of Interior, Bureau of Reclamation, *Annual Project History, North Platte Project,* Vol. 15, 1927

Wyoming State Parks & Historic Sites Digital Collections Guernsey Museum Digitization Project *Tabulations of Main Developments*

Newspapers

Boston Evening Transcript, January 3, 1935

Boston Evening Transcript, November 2, 1936

Iron Gazette, Hartville Wyoming, Volume 1, Number 1, November 17, 1899

Torrington Telegram, July 19, 1934
F S Today, Williams, Gerald W., *The Civilian Conservation Corps and National Forests – Looking Back Forest Service History,* March, 21, 2008

Unpublished Sources

CC Worker Statue Plaque, at the Guernsey State Park Museum

Museum Plaque, located south of Museum, placed by Wyoming State Parks and Historic Sites

Snyder, Jim, Unpublished notes attached to Trail Map E, 1987

Snyder, Jim, Unpublished Notes with Bureau of Reclamation Maps, Guernsey Wyoming 1991 (Jim, for many years was the curator at the Museum)

Waring, Neil, unpublished work, *42 Years In Front of the Class, from 1991 notes, 2012*

Waring, Neil, Wyoming History Teaching Notes, Unpublished, 1970-2012

Web Sources

Belli, Anthony M., Lost Treasure Online, *Lost Treasure, Slade's Long Lost Loot,*
http://www.losttreasure.com/content/archives/sta
te-treasure-wyoming**,** January, 2000

Civilian Conservation Corps Legacy
http://www.ccclegacy.org

Civilian Conservation Corps Legacy, *CCC Camps Wyoming,*
www.ccclegacy.org/ccc.camps.wyoming.htr

Civilian Conservation Corps Legacy, *Passing the Legacy To Future Generations,* CCC a Brief History –
The Program Had Great Support
http://www.ccclegacy.org/CCC_Brief_History.html

Gonzel, Bill - Gonzel Group, *Wessels Living History Farm, Farming in the 1930s*
http://www.livinghistoryfarm.org/farminginthe30s
/farminginthe1930s.html

Guernsey State Park Auto Tour, Guernsey Dam,
http://www.usbr.gov/projects/PrintFacilityAttribut
es.jsp?fac_Name=Guernsey Dam

History Online,
http://www.nps.gov/history/history/online_books
/rusticarch/part3.htm

History.com, http://www.history.com/this-day-in-
history/fdr-creates-civilian-conservation-corps ---4
http://www.justinMuseum.com/famjustin/cccback
.html

http://www.mountainproject.com/v/area-3-the-
revolutionary-climbing-wall-of-dead-mans-
gulch/107461853 introduction.htm
Justin Family Museum,

Justin, James F., *Civilian Conservation Corps Facts
– Lest We Forget,* Civilian Conservation Corps
Museum

Lost Treasures Wyoming,
http://www.losttreasure.com/content/archives/sta
te-treasure-wyoming

Mountain Project,
http://www.mountainproject.com/v/area-3-the-
revolutionary-climbing-wall-of-dead-mans-
gulch/107461853

National Park Service Rustic Architecture,
Roosevelt's Emergency Programs 1933-1935, 1-10
http://www.cr.nps.gov/history/online_books/rusti
carch/

Park Net - National Park Service, *Parkitecture In Western National Parks, Early Twentieth Century Rustic Design & Naturalism,* *http://www.nps.gov/hdp/exhibits/parkitect*

Peters, John T., Gerhard and Woolley, *The American Presidency Project, Roosevelt,* online edition *2013* http://www.usbr.gov/pmts/hydraulics_lab/pubs/HL/HL-2012-04.pdf

Wyoming State Parks and Historic Sites Guernsey State Park, http://wyoparks.state.wy.us

Wyoming State Parks and Historic Sites, *Guernsey Museum Digitization Project,* http://wyoshpo.state.wy.us/westerntrails/stateparks.html.

List of Illustrations by Page Numbers

60. Building the front archway of the Museum*

61. Inspecting inside of partially built Museum*

62. Museum Display

62. Museum Floor

63. Women's Restroom door – Museum

64. Steps from lower lot to Museum

65. Museum view South-wing

66. Museum – View from lower parking lot

67. Stone culvert – one of several in the park

68. BR-9 Educational Building*

70. Nine Mule Deer

71. Castle Southwest view

72. Davis Bay

73. Super Moon over Mae West Hill

74. Camp BR-10*

75. Train passing under bridge on Skyline Drive

76. Newell Bay

77. Newell Bay steps

79. Brimmer Point Lookout – the Point

80. Brimmer Point trail Foot Bridge.

80. The view from Brimmer Point

81. CCC painted labels on Brimmer Point fence

82. Fence hold-down

83. Distant view of Brimmer Point

84. Steps to nowhere

85. Echo Cave – words on the wall

86. Echo Cave Trail

87. View from Echo Cave

88. Echo Cave – Photo from Lakeshore Drive

89. Pull-off view on Skyline Drive

90. CCC Limestone Quarry

91. Westside trail/map sign

92. Log marker for Tunnel Mountain Trail

93. North Bluff Castle

94. Laramie Peak from the Castle

95. View through the Castle arches

96. Million Dollar Biffy

97. Fireplace on hill near Davis Bay

99. Oregon Trail Ruts south of Guernsey

101. BR-10 Powderhouse

101. Walking Trail and floor from old Camp BR-10

102. Foundations of old Camp BR-10

105. Men of Camp 10 – Supper line*

106. BR-10 Commander Maxwell*

107. BR-9 Superintendent Coffman*

110. Fish rearing pond work south of Guernsey*

111. Young man fishing at Island Park – summer 2012

112. Old Head Gate at Island Park

114. Landscaping crew*

114. CCC fireplace cut from natural park stone

167. Historic photo of the Sunrise Iron Ore Mine**

168. Early train**

170. The Dam- Photo 2013 from Round Top Mountain

172. Working on dam summer 2013

173. Spillway

174. High water pool – west side

175. Dam and Powerplant Plaque on Gatehouse

176. Gatehouse

177. Walkers on the New CCC roadway atop the Dam**

177. South Side Gates

178. Full Lake – Summer 2014

180. Sandy Beach

181. Yurts

182. Turkey - Mule Deer

183. Egret below the dam

184. Vultures on the Roost and in the air

185. Bald Eagles

189. CCC Worker Statue

191. Museum View from the South

192. Sitting Bull Shelter – View

193. Laramie Peak from the Castle

194. Million Dollar Biffy

195. Sandy Beach

196. Marsh Mountain Trail

197. Red Cliff Trail Steps

198. Yurts

199. Register Cliff and the Ruts

200. View West from Brimmer Point at sundown

201. Powderhouse off Lakeshore Drive

202. Camp–10 Remains

203. Lakeshore Drive View

204. Mule Deer - Turkey

205. Cottontail - Robin

206. Ducks taking flight - Woodpecker

207. Canadian Geese - Merganser

208. Blue Jay - Mule Deer

209. Cormorants – Great Blue Herons

210. Cedar Waxwing - Bald Eagle

243. Neil Waring on Marsh Mt. Trail

*Historic Photos used with permission and my utmost thanks, **Courtesy of Wyoming State Archives, Department of State Parks and Cultural Resources**.

** Historic photos from my personal collection are from my 42 years as a history teacher. These photos are, to the best of my knowledge, not copyrighted. If any of the photos are copyright protected I will be glad to remove or cite them as per copyright if contacted by the holder of the copyright.

Index

The Author taking a break on Marsh Mountain Trail

About the Author

Neil Waring, born in O'Neill, Nebraska and raised in Fairbury, Nebraska was educated at Peru State College, Wayne State College and the University of Wyoming. He spent 42 years in education, teaching, American History, Wyoming History, and Geography along with a variety of other social science and English classes. Although the majority of his teaching career was spent teaching at the high school level he also taught Wyoming History, as an adjunct professor, for area community colleges for nearly twenty years.

In addition to this book Mr. Waring has published short stories and historical pieces online and in print. He writes a popular Wyoming blog, Wyoming Fact and Fiction, at http://wyoming-fact-and-fiction.blogspot.com and can be followed on Twitter @wyohistoryguy.

Writing of this book also inspired Neil to start another blog, this one about Guernsey State Park. http://visitguernseystatepark.blogspot.com.

He has a historical fiction book, set in and around Fort Laramie, scheduled to be released in the summer of 2015 and two children's, growing up books, found on Amazon.com, *Melvin the E Street Ghost,* and, *Then Mike Said, There's a Zombie in My Basement.*

Neil and his wife Jan live in Guernsey, Wyoming near Fort Laramie, the Oregon Trail, and Guernsey State Park. When not writing Mr. Waring spends his time with building projects, reading, gardening, playing golf, photography and hiking.

Made in the USA
Columbia, SC
26 August 2018